The Road to GUMPTION

Using Your Inner Courage to Balance Your Work and Personal Life

Gary Lim, M.A.

DORATO PRESS

Dedicated to my wife Judy, who not only travels with me

on the Road to Gumption, but whose encouragement

first put me on the Road to start with.

Publisher's Cataloging-in-Publication Data
Lim, Gary.
The road to gumption : using your inner courage to balance your work
and personal life / Gary Lim – Rev. ed.
p. cm.
1. Happiness. 2. Change (Psychology). I. Title.

BF575.H27 2007
158.1—dc21   LCCN: 2007927948

For further information:

315-885-1532

www.RoadToGumption.com

gump•tion (gŭmp'shən) *n. Informal.*
1. Boldness of enterprise; initiative
or aggressiveness.   **2.** Guts; spunk.

Author's Note: About This Book

Available time appears to be getting increasingly scarce. In today's age of being constantly connected, by Bluetooth cell phones, instant messaging, voicemail, email, Blackberries, Treos, Qs, and other devices yet to be invented, the boundaries between work and personal lives risk becoming blurred.

As connected as we are through technology advances, balancing our work and our LOAF (my acronym for "loved ones and family") time is an increasing challenge. Though work allows us the cash flow to do things with our families and loved ones, if those work priorities take up too much time, there is no time left for LOAFing. As one overworked professional once told me glumly, "All the money in the world doesn't do me much good if I have no time to spend it with my family."

And yet we must continue to make that income, to pay the bills and provide for our lifestyles. The real question becomes what is that "right" level of lifestyle? The answer is highly individual and might require making a significant change in order to balance work and LOAF priorities.

Creating change and achieving success requires being open to dealing with uncertainty, and taking risks – in short, **it takes gumption** to change and succeed. Change is scary, but there's nothing wrong with recognizing that fact.

Your ability to embrace change will help you figure out the path to your goals. During the journey you might even discover new goals that are perhaps more timely or relevant. Reach your goals and you will live your dreams; though never perfect, it's a great life.

Surprisingly enough, if you meet your goals you face risk. Like it or not, there may be some people around you, maybe even some very close to you, who would not be as supportive as you think about your success. Your successes might make them feel left behind, and so you might find that they behave differently around you. They might even complain that you're the one who is "not like you used to be."

And you wouldn't be like you used to be – having gumption is all about being able to make changes, and about taking risks that will move you closer to balancing your work and LOAF priorities. *The Road to Gumption* is a reminder that this journey is challenging, perpetual, and is one that takes courage, but the feelings and the ups and downs you experience will be quite expected. You're not alone – but many times it will definitely feel like you are.

In this parable that takes place in the fictional town of "Gumption," our traveler, from his home region of "The City" and "City Sprawl," discovers the town's spirit of gumption through some of its residents and their "Rules of Gumption." He leaves with a renewed sense of perspective, self-discovery, and purpose.

The Rules of Gumption are divided into 5 phases that I call **The 5 P's of Change**, laying a roadmap that can help you get to where you want to be:

- **Prepare** – mentally prepare to make a change
- **Plan** – create a plan for your change
- **Pursue** – implement the plan, pursue your goals
- **Persevere** – stick to it, through the rough spots
- **Positive** – keep your spirits up; stay positive

I hope you, too, will find *The Road to Gumption* full of useful rules and reminders, so you can reach out and successfully work towards your dreams, whatever they may be. And may that allow you to have as much time as you want for LOAFing around!

Gary Lim
info@RoadToGumption.com

Contents

The Traveler

As John prepared to leave for his sixth business trip in as many weeks, the conversation with his wife Shelly started to get tense again. He was standing by the bed, packing his bag for the long drive out of state. Shelly, looking at the back of her husband's head, said curtly, "So when *are* we going to have the time to discuss these things?"

"I told you, when I get back at the end of the week," said John, shaking his head without turning around, clearly annoyed.

"But when you get home, you're usually exhausted – completely beat. Then you don't want to have any heavy discussions." Shelly was not the only one getting tired of treading old ground.

"You know how my schedule is," complained John, almost throwing his folded slacks into the suitcase. "During this time of the year the job has me pretty much on the road from Tuesday through Friday. Could be worse – my territory could be bigger."

"I know, I know." Shelly folded her arms and leaned against the doorframe. "But we're going to have to talk about our lives sometime. We hardly have time to eat together – what happened to balancing our lives and trying to plan for kids? Sometimes I feel like we're on a big treadmill."

"Well *excuse me* for creating such an inconvenience!" John turned to glare at her, his face starting to flush as his voice jumped a few decibels. "It takes money to provide for a balanced lifestyle and kids, you know!" He was practically shouting now.

"Yeah, but what good is it if we don't have any time or energy left to do anything?!" Shelly was irritated too. She and John had gone around and around on this topic before, with John usually being the reluctant one to discuss things. "That's what I mean about a treadmill – are we going to continue working our butts off, making good money, but having almost no time to enjoy it?"

John threw the last of his shirts into his bag, and zipped it closed in sullen silence. He didn't have an answer to that question. His and his wife's schedules were hectic, with the two of them seeing each other only from Friday night until Monday or Tuesday morning. And though he didn't like to admit it, Shelly was right, when he was home, he was often too tired to talk about heavy subjects. Sometimes he was too tired to talk, period.

John straightened up, bag in hand, and looked angrily at his wife. "Well, as usual, I have no answer to your usually unanswerable questions!" He brushed by her and stalked out of the bedroom, heading for the kitchen.

Shelly caught up with him by the sink and put a hand on his arm. In a suddenly more conciliatory tone, she said, "Look, dear, I know it's not a great time to talk about this …"

"It's *never* a great time when you waylay me with this, just as I'm heading out the door on another trip!" John interrupted explosively.

"So then when *are* we going to talk about our future?!" Shelly, angered again by John's tone, found her own voice rising. "You always say there are no answers, but we can't even decide what the questions are!"

Turning to look at his wife, John could only stare at her in frustration. Suddenly, it was as if the resolve went out of his body, and his shoulders slumped. He looked at the floor, took a deep breath, then replied in a quieter voice, "Okay, I guess we ought to talk after I get back from this trip on Friday night. I mean, let's make sure we talk about it this weekend."

Surprised by her husband's sudden change of demeanor, Shelly said in a much calmer tone, "Okay, dear, let's do that. We both probably have a lot to think about before then."

John snapped his head up and stared at his wife. "Oh, and what's that supposed to mean?" he asked in an accusing tone, sounding combative again. "Are you trying to tell me something?"

"Geez, no!" exclaimed Shelly, instantly irritated once more by the emotional mood swings of their conversation. "I just meant that we both have to do a lot of thinking about what we want to do, and how we get there! This is making me mad!" She shook her head and threw up her hands in frustration.

"Well, I certainly don't want to be the cause of you getting mad!" retorted John sarcastically. "So why don't

I just remove the source of trouble, and be on my way right now!" He grabbed his bag and laptop case, and headed towards the door to the garage.

"C'mon, John, let's not be this way," said Shelly as her husband passed through the doorframe into the garage.

The door between the kitchen and the garage slammed, and a minute later, she heard his car start up, then back out. As the garage door lowered, Shelly realized that this was the first time he'd gone on a trip without them saying goodbye to each other.

She leaned against the kitchen counter, looked out the window, and took a deep breath, exhaling slowly. Not good, she thought, but she was angry, frustrated, and upset all at once. She couldn't help but wonder if this was the beginning of the end.

The garage door lowered, as John backed out into the street, fast, without really looking. Fortunately, no other vehicles or people were around. He threw the car into Drive and took off, tires squealing at first.

"That really ticks me off," he muttered under his breath. He fumed about the parting shouting match he had with Shelly, and found himself gripping the steering wheel tightly.

Commute habits soon took over, and he clicked on the radio, tuning first to a news station. "Traffic's really backed up around the interchange right now," warned the traffic reporter. "There's a report of an accident that's just occurred. Try to take alternate routes if you can."

As he headed for a different entrance onto the freeway, John tried to move beyond the feelings of irritation and frustration that he felt. But he couldn't help replay the last few minutes of conversation in his mind. Though he was frustrated with Shelly for trying to pin him down to talking about things, he had to admit privately that he wasn't sure what they would talk about. He just didn't know what the future held, so how could he talk about it with her? He didn't even know if he'd still be at the same job a year from now, or two, or three.

The usually long and boring five-and-a-half hour drive that lay ahead of him didn't seem like it was going to be boring this time. Long still, but not boring – he was steamed, all right.

"What does Shelly expect?" he muttered to himself. "I don't even know how secure my job is, so how in the world can we talk about when we'll have kids? Can't talk about kids until we know things are more secure and predictable." John found his frustration level rising again.

He turned onto the access ramp, negotiated the merge, and headed out of the city limits. Once he cleared the city, he'd be on open roads for awhile, passing only small towns here and there. As traffic thinned, he brought the sedan up to cruising speed, kicked in the cruise control, and took his foot off the pedal. The big car cruised on into the afternoon.

The miles and hours passed by, with John alternately listening to the radio to distract himself, but still thinking about the argument he'd had with Shelly. There wouldn't be much to talk about at the end of the week, he thought. We'll have to agree to put off planning for kids until our financial situation is more ideal.

Though he and Shelly were not by nature an extravagant couple, they did have their expenses. Because of their busy schedules, they ate out a lot, adding significantly to their overhead. And they lived in an area of the country where housing costs were among the highest, but that was certainly not something they could control. They also took nice vacations when they could, staying in the nicest hotels and dining at great restaurants.

They deserved those breaks, as hard as they both worked, John reasoned. You have to enjoy some of the fruits of your labors.

By now John had reached the more isolated part of his route. The highway he was on had two lanes in each direction, with curves and scenic views now and then. At times the highway split, with the lanes of the opposite direction out of sight. Most of the towns with names he saw on the destination signs seemed to be off-road somewhere, not visible from the highway. He idly wondered what it was like to live in those towns.

Probably not a very exciting life, he thought, as he made some guesses about what those people might do for a living.

Suddenly, the big sedan shuddered, as the car hit something on the road. The cruise control disengaged, the car started to slow, and John found himself struggling to keep the vehicle on a straight path. As he brought the car to a stop on the shoulder, he realized that one of his tires must have blown.

Getting out of the car, he walked around it and soon found the problem. The right rear tire had a big construction nail in it. No problem getting it repaired, he figured, but with only a temporary spare, he couldn't drive very far, or very fast. He'd have to get that tire fixed in a nearby town somewhere.

After putting on what seemed like the smallest spare tire known to man, John loaded the flat tire into the trunk. He jumped back in the car, started it up, and merged back onto the road, looking for the nearest exit. After about 15 miles, he saw an exit sign. It showed the name of a town 7 miles away, but the sign was quite weather-beaten and some of the letters had been worn away. It looked something like this:

Gս н ᵂon   7

He turned off the highway and headed for the town, driving down a quiet two-lane road. Dusk was starting to settle, heightened by tall densely-leafed trees on both sides of the road. About 7 miles from where he first drove onto the access road, it started to curve to the right. As he rounded the bend, the sign for the town came into view, lit by his headlights in the falling darkness:

WELCOME TO GUMPTION
Population 1,745

"A town called Gumption?" John muttered to himself, "Yeah right." He drove down the street, looking for a gas station or other repair place. It seemed like everything was closed.

Pulling into the parking lot in front of what looked like a small hotel, he got out of the car, locked it, and went in the front door. He found himself in the lobby of the hotel, and at the desk a pleasant-looking woman looked up from her newspaper. She smiled as John approached.

"Hello," said John, "I hope you can help me. I was on the freeway, and picked up a nail in my tire. I need to get it fixed soon, since I've only got a temporary spare. Can anyone here in town fix it for me?"

"Probably not tonight, I'm afraid," said the woman. She gestured in the general direction of down the street. "The man who owns the auto repair shop here is out of town because of a family emergency. He won't be back until tomorrow morning."

"Well, how far is it to the next major town where I can get this fixed?"

"I'm not quite sure ..." started the woman, pursing her lips. "Maybe 75 miles or so, towards The City? I don't really go there that often, and my husband usually drives."

Oh man, that's backtracking towards home, thought John. I may be stuck here for tonight. What a terrific way to start a trip. First a big blow-up with Shelly, and now this – stuck in some lousy small town.

"Do you know what time he'll be back?" John asked the woman.

"I think he said he'd be back around 8:30 or 9 in the morning. Do you think you might need a room?" the woman asked eagerly, with the prospect of an unexpected sale looming.

What choice do I have, thought John glumly, can't drive 75 miles at a slow speed, in the wrong direction, and chance something else happening in the dead of night. "Well, I guess so, if you have any availability. And are there any restaurants around?"

"Yes, and yes," she said brightly. "We're not that full at all tonight, being low season right now. There's a good restaurant almost next door, that's also kind of like our gathering place here in town."

After registering and getting a key, John went to his car and got his things. Unlocking the room with the key, he entered and saw that it wasn't all that different from what he'd seen at a dozen other business hotels, but maybe a little cozier. He dropped his bags on the bed, and fished for his cell phone.

Locating the speed dial for his home, he hesitated for just a second, remembering the note that he and his wife had parted on. He pushed "Talk."

"Hi Shelly, it's me," John said after he heard his wife's voice answer. His tone was flat, neither warm nor hostile.

"Hi John." Same flatness. They were both still tense from the conversation hours ago.

"I was just calling to tell you that one of my tires blew on the freeway."

"Oh no!" exclaimed Shelly, her voice instantly showing concern. "Are you all right? Where are you now?"

"I'm in a small town called Gumption, believe it or not," replied John, somewhat exasperated by the recent developments. "I have to get the tire fixed tomorrow morning, so I checked into what's probably their only hotel here. What a lousy break – I'm going to have to reschedule all my morning appointments tomorrow." John could feel his stress level rising again.

After a few more minutes of conversation with his wife, John ended the call by saying he would call her the next morning after he got underway again. Neither mentioned the fight they had earlier, and both stuck to the topic of the call. Shelly told him to take care, but it was clear that she was still taut about what happened earlier in the day.

Slipping the phone back in his pocket, John headed downstairs, through the lobby, and out onto the sidewalk, looking for the restaurant. To his left, across the parking lot, he caught a glimpse of a lit sign, *Food for Thought*. He headed for it.

Upon entering, he was quickly seated in a booth, and, looking around, saw that there weren't many people in the restaurant. Might as well make the best of it tonight, he thought miserably, as he opened the menu. He was stressed and irritated indeed.

The Journey of Revelation Begins

"Hi there, how are you tonight? My name is Carol, and I'll be your server," the waitress, another pleasant-looking woman, greeted John. "May I bring you something to drink?"

"Well, a glass of white wine would be great for starters," said John. He wondered if everyone in this town was pleasant-looking. The servers at some of the restaurants he and Shelly frequented in City Sprawl usually wore bored or harried expressions. He finished checking out the menu and put it down. A few minutes later, the server returned with his wine, and John was ready to order.

After he got his dinner order squared away, he turned his attention to the dining room décor. Hanging on the walls were a variety of frames containing quotes. Some of the frames with quotes were made of shiny brass, making them stand out from the others. Interspersed among the quotes were framed pictures of people, presumably some of those who originally uttered the quotes. The frame hanging on the wall of his booth said, "I once shot an elephant in my pajamas. What he was doing in my pajamas, I'll never know." He recognized it as a Groucho Marx quote.

Carol came back with John's salad and put it in front of him, along with a basket of biscuits. "Interesting looking place," said John. "So the quotes are the 'food for thought'? Is this a chain, or a locally owned restaurant?"

"Locally owned," answered Carol, "by yours truly and my husband!" She did a mock curtsy.

"Well it's very nice." John grinned, as the wine began to take the edge off a bit. He started to poke at his salad. "How long have you had it? Did you buy it, or start it?"

"We started it a little over two years ago, when we first moved here from The City."

John looked up in surprise. "Yeah? I live in that area now! I'm in City Sprawl."

"Well, we were practically neighbors, then!" Carol laughed. "It was getting way too crowded and stressed for us, and we were looking for a change in our lifestyle." She leaned her shoulder on the edge of the booth across from John and folded her arms. "I was working in retail as a store manager, and my husband Greg – that's him you see in the kitchen – was customer service director at another City firm. We just spent too much time working and worrying."

"So what's the connection with moving up here?" asked John as he picked up a forkful of salad.

"None really – we didn't know anyone here, but we'd stopped over on the way to our vacation spot a couple of times before," Carol replied, adjusting her shirt sleeves and pushing them up a little higher. "We always enjoyed the ambience in this town, though it's seasonal. Much busier during summer and winter vacation season, and holidays. You're catching us at an off time. What brings you here?"

"Unscheduled stop," said John, talking with his mouth full of salad. "I got a flat tire on the highway and am running on a temporary spare. The lady at the hotel told me there's a guy locally who can fix it, but he's away until tomorrow morning."

"Yes, I did hear that Todd – the guy with the repair shop – had to go visit his mother, kind of last-minute notice. Where are you headed?"

"From my home in City Sprawl, to the Big City in the Next State," said John. "It's almost a six-hour drive." He put his fork down, took a sip of wine, and proceeded to tell Carol about his job and the sales territory that he covered, including the amount of travel he'd had to do lately.

"Sounds familiar." Carol sighed. "It's weird, when we still lived in The City, it seemed like we had so little time to ourselves, too. That's why we started to think that we needed to make a change." She looked up as a couple of arriving customers entered the dining room. "Oops, back to work – I'll check back with you in a few. I hope you like your salad – the greens are really good today!"

Turning again to his salad, John grinned wryly. The wine was starting to make him feel a lot more relaxed than he was when he first rolled into town. Fresh greens indeed, he thought, and I've been getting too used to 5-day-old bagged salad, hardly touched, at the bottom of the crisper drawer in the fridge.

As he ate, he wondered what it would be like to live in a town like this. Less than 2,000 people, small downtown area – didn't seem like there'd be much to do. But he was curious about why Carol and her family would move from The City to this little town, and wondered how they were able to adjust to it. How could you possibly make the same kind of living here as you would in City Sprawl or The City?

Midway through his salad, John looked up and saw the man from the kitchen approaching.

"Hi there, how are you? I'm Greg, Carol's husband and partner in this fine establishment." Greg stuck his hand out with a smile. "I hear you live near where we used to live!" John shook hands, exchanging the greeting.

"You know, now I'm really curious about how you and your wife decided to move here," said John. "This must be very different than living in The City. That is, if you don't mind me asking."

"Not at all! It definitely is different," said Greg, gesturing to indicate the surroundings. "And that's what's terrific about it! We have a really nice life here – I mean, not that life was terrible before, but we can now really appreciate the things that are important to us."

"But, going from a region with over two million people to a town with less than two thousand? Was that a culture shock, or what?" asked John, picking up his salad fork again.

"You'd think so," said Greg with a grin. "And in some ways it was, but actually we were prepared for it – it became our goal after awhile."

"You mean, you planned for this?" John raised his eyebrows, waving the glass of wine in his hand.

"More or less – Carol and I wanted a change. We were tired of jostling with a million people, at work, on the freeways, during the commute, at the mall parking lots 4 days before Christmas – you know the drill, you live there. So we started a process of discussing what we really wanted as part of our lifestyle, and what we didn't want. It was that first step that helped us on our way."

"First step?" asked John.

"Yeah," said Greg, slipping into the booth seat across from John and warming to the topic. "Like that quote hanging on the wall over there." He pointed to a framed quote nearby, as John turned his head to look.

A journey of a thousand miles begins with a single step.
(--Chinese philosopher Lao-Tzu)

"Our first 'single step' was for Carol and I to have a really honest discussion about what we liked about our lives, and what we didn't like. Believe it or not, we actually had never done that before – we were just too busy trying to figure out how to cope with the lifestyle we already had."

"I know how that feels," agreed John, stabbing at the last of his salad with his fork. He had a memory flashback to the fight he and Shelly had earlier in the day.

Greg watched John skewer the last few pieces of lettuce with his fork, and continued. "Well, what we found was that we were definitely worried about our ability to affect the quality of our personal lives, but had been unwilling to face up to it. It was kind of a scary discussion at first, where you feel almost like you're going down a path with no way out. After all, what if we discussed all the things we didn't like, then did nothing, or didn't know what to do? It would be like shining a spotlight on what we didn't like, then trying to get on with life."

"How long did this discussion last?" asked John, reaching for another cheddar biscuit from the basket on the table.

"The better part of a year, on and off," replied Greg. "We just kept coming back to the topic, discussing more and different aspects of it." He grinned at the sight of John wolfing down the biscuit in three bites. "Those are good, aren't they?"

Carol came up to the table, looked at Greg, and said, "Okay, Chef, back to work. We have hungry customers waiting!" Greg got up from the booth and looked at John. "I'll catch you in a bit, okay? Carol – I was just telling John about when we first examined our lifestyle and tried to figure out what we wanted."

"Oh, that long and drawn-out discussion," Carol said with a laugh. "Okay, I'll continue the story – but get going – we have a sirloin and a salmon to serve! Need the steak still mooing…"

As Greg headed back to the kitchen, Carol turned to John and said, "Are you finished with your salad? And where did he leave off?"

"He was saying that you discussed the pro's and con's of The City Area for about a year, on and off." John held his plate up.

Taking the empty plate, Carol said, "Yes, we did. We weren't sure if we were going to talk ourselves into a deeper state of funk, because we didn't know how we'd feel about changing things." John nodded.

"But as Greg and I started to realize what we wanted out of life, we also started to think that we probably would have to take a chance to try to achieve it. I think that deep inside we knew that if we did nothing, kept going down the same path, things would probably remain the same."

"Had either of you lived in smaller towns or cities before?" asked John, taking another sip of his wine.

"No, neither of us had," said Carol. "Both Greg and I grew up in different cities, but they're similar to The City in size and activities. And for the longest time, I think we both thought that we'd never want to live anywhere but in places like The City."

"So when did you first start thinking that moving to a place like this might be a possibility?" asked John, as he drained the last of his glass of wine.

Carol looked up as another couple entered the dining room and sat down. "Just a sec, let me tend to my new customers. Do you want another glass of wine?

Tell you what, it's on the house. Be right back." She took his wine glass and salad plate and disappeared.

Left to his thoughts for a few, John mused over what he heard. He thought, no way Shelly and I could move to a place like this. We'd probably miss all the things there are to do in City Sprawl and The City.

It didn't occur to John that for the past few months he and his wife hadn't had much time to do anything in The City. Except perhaps to go out to eat after yet another exhausting day or week.

He looked around the dining room again, scanning the walls. To the right, he spotted one of the shiny brass frames, with a quote which read:

Rule #1: Start with a small step – any step.

The quote was not attributed to any author or famous person. John thought about what Greg had said about taking the first step and discussing what he and his wife were looking for. Just then, Carol walked up with a new glass of wine, and put it on the table.

"Hey, I notice that there are some quotes which seem to be numbered rules, like that Rule #1 over there," said John. "Whose rules are those?"

Carol grinned and looked at him. "Those are our rules," she said with a chuckle.

John picked up the wine glass and looked at her over the rim. "What do you mean, 'your rules'?"

Carol smiled and gestured inclusively. "Rules that we came up with, based on our story and others who live here. You see, there are a few other people here who also made big changes by moving here. A number of folks who weren't that different from Greg and me a few years ago, and probably you now."

"Whaddya mean, 'me now'?" asked John in mock indignation. He took another sip of his new glass of wine. "Thank you for the wine, by the way."

"You're welcome." Carol laughed then perched on the edge of the seat across from John and said, "What I mean is, people like us who thought we'd never make as drastic a change in our lifestyles as we did. Comfortable in what we were doing, yet sometimes thinking, is this all there is? Is this all there's going to be? Anyway, the rules are the results of lots of exchanging stories between some of the newer residents of Gumption. I suppose you could call them the Rules of Gumption!" Carol laughed again.

She continued, "Rule #1 refers to the first step we took of discussing what we really wanted out of life. If we continued to ignore our gnawing thoughts, we wouldn't be standing here." She looked up across the room and jumped to her feet. "Oops, gotta run again – but your dinner will be along soon!"

No more than a minute or two after Carol took off, Greg showed up at John's booth again, holding a bowl of soup. "Hey John, help me out," said Greg with a smile, "try out my new French Onion soup and tell me what you think."

John looked up at him and said, "Now how did you know that I love a good French Onion soup?" He tried a spoonful, and gave the thumbs-up sign.

Then he asked, "So Greg, Carol told me Rule #1 over there is from your experience. What are some of the other 'Rules of Gumption'?"

"First, there's a point I want to make about that first rule," said Greg. He propped his shoe on the edge of the bench across from John, and rested his elbow on his knee. "A lot of people, Carol and I included, sometimes get stuck worrying about which first step to take. About whether it was the right first step, and so on. And then you get so worried about whether that step is the right one, you don't take any step at all. So the idea is to take a small step, any step, so you can get going. If it's the wrong step, you can fix it later."

"That makes sense," agreed John, savoring another spoonful of the French Onion soup.

"There are a couple of thoughts you can keep in mind to help get through that first step," Greg continued. "One of them is to acknowledge what you want to change, and be energized by it instead of being put off."

"That also makes sense," said John, as he wiped the corner of his mouth with his napkin. "But that almost sounds easier than it is."

"It definitely was harder than we thought," agreed Greg, "because at first Carol and I really didn't know how we were going to address our need for change."

John stopped eating for a moment and furrowed his brow in thought. "I'm not sure I know what you mean," he said, looking at Greg.

"We imagined our ideal setting and environment, with our desire to have kids and all, but we didn't know how we were going to achieve that in The City Area," answered Greg. "So all we had at the end of our self-realization phase was a challenge of trying to figure out what to do about it."

"And that's just the point!" concluded Greg as he stabbed his forefinger in the air for emphasis. "Realizing that our next step was to figure out our next step, meant we were on our way somewhere. It's like we realized that we were taking action, figuring a plan. That's what energized us."

He looked up as a man, walking into the dining room, called out, "Hey Greg, what's up?" The newcomer came over and shook hands.

"Hey Doug, how's it going?" said Greg. "Say hello to John – he lives in The City Area."

John shook hands with Doug, a fairly big man, as the latter said, "Oh yeah? My old haunts in a former life, too! What brings you here?"

John explained the circumstances that led to his arrival in Gumption. "So, are you another guy who's made a big change by coming here, like Greg and Carol?" he asked Doug.

"Yup, in more ways than one!" Doug laughed, patting his belly. "Believe it or not, this svelte body used to have a bit more baggage on it, until recently. I used to love anything sweet, particularly donuts and cookies. My last name's Vita, you know, so everyone used to call me 'Dolce' … like Dolce Vita." He laughed again.

"What did you used to do in The City, and how'd you end up here?" asked John, finishing the last spoonful of the soup.

"Was a tech support rep," answered Doug. "Sitting in front of those computers all day, on the phone, didn't do my athletic body any good!" He laughed loudly, looking at Greg. Doug was proving to be a jolly one.

"Hey, I need to run back to the kitchen and see where John's dinner is," said Greg. "I have Joe helping me tonight, and he's gonna think I'm slacking off. You guys chat a bit." He headed back to the kitchen.

Gesturing to the bench that Greg just vacated, John said to Doug, "What brought you here? You didn't know Greg from before did you?"

"Oh no, but it was the same type of thing, in retrospect," said Doug, sliding into the seat. "I first ran across this place coming and going to my summer rental up at the resort. Always thought it was a kind of a quaint place. And a good bakery, too!" He grinned broadly and rubbed his stomach. "Then I started to get tired of what I was doing. Tech support work is interesting, but after a while it's all the same story of long hours, troubleshooting problems, things like that. And sometimes, after a long stint of trying to solve a technical problem, we'd find that it was the user's fault, something they screwed up, but never bothered to tell us about. Man, what a waste of time!"

"So what did you do? Have a talk with your family about the meaning of life?" asked John with a wry smile.

"Actually, it was just me and the cat," answered Doug with a chuckle. "My ex-wife split from me a couple of years before. Said I was spending too much time working, and getting overweight doing so." His smile faded, and he paused, momentarily lost in thought. "She certainly had a point, there. So I decided to go on a weight loss kick, and started thinking about what I was looking to do. Even if I left the company and went to another one, I'd be doing the same type of thing, with the same kind of hours – more of the same all around."

"What do you do here?" asked John, pushing his empty soup bowl to the side.

Doug laughed again; he certainly was a jovial guy. "Well, since I love sweets, I bought the bakery here that I had admired so much! Baking has always been a hobby of mine, believe it or not."

"But I had to reach a realization about something. Did these guys mention to you about the first step, and how you want to be energized by what you want to change?"

John nodded and pointed to the wall. "They told me about Rule of Gumption #1 on the wall there."

"Well, there's a flip side of being energized about what you want to change. You also have to figure out what you can't change, and be able to live with it and work with it." Doug looked at John with a serious expression.

Then Doug's face broke into a big grin again. "I know I can't change lovin' donuts, so I decided to work with them!" He laughed uproariously at his own humor.

John, grinning, shook his head and asked, "How did you lose the weight and keep it off? Sounds like you've got enough temptation to the contrary."

"You know what I found when I moved to this place?" said Doug, eyebrows raised in wonderment. "That I had a lot more time to think about getting exercise, and that I was happier and more energetic, so I could do the exercise. I have to get up early so I can get the baked goods on the shelves, but I really like what I'm doing. I didn't know how much the other job was affecting me, I really didn't."

Carol walked up with a plate, and saw Doug. "Oh hi there, Doug, how are you? Did you bring me some of my favorite donuts?" She put the plate down in front of John. "There you are, sir, your dinner – Beluga Caviar, Dom Perignon, and twin filets of beef."

John looked at his plate, under the table, then at Carol and said, "Well, the last one, anyway, but I don't see the first two items anywhere." They all laughed.

"I was just telling him about how I got here," said Doug to Carol. "And about how I love working with donuts!"

"You finish your story then, I'll be back. Do you want anything, Doug?" asked Carol. Doug shook his head. "Okay, bon appetit, John." Off she went again.

"Please, go ahead and eat," said Doug, "I'll just continue chattering here. Actually the interesting thing about having to acknowledge what you can't change is that it holds many people back. They look at something that they can't change, and they let that stand in the way of making a change. I was that way for a while, too. I would be thinking, man, I can't lose this weight, I come from a family of heavyset people – it's in my genes."

He patted his belly again and said, "It's in my jeans, all right!" grinning broadly. "But then I started to realize, okay, so I have my family's thighs, so what? It's not like there's a family specification that says the thighs had to be a certain size. I can do this – I may not ever look like Russell Crowe or Brad Pitt, but I can certainly lose a lot of the luggage I'd acquired around my middle over the past few years, sitting in front of computers, being on the phone, and not getting much exercise."

John looked at him, listening carefully, while eating bites of his filet mignon. "So that's what you did, then? Lost the weight?"

"Uh-huh, dropped about 70 pounds so far, in a little over a year," said Doug proudly. "And, I've dropped those pounds while being completely surrounded by donuts, cake, and cookies!" He laughed heartily again, slapping the table, rattling John's wine glass slightly.

"What's all this noise going on?" asked Carol with a smile, appearing again from around the corner. She looked at Doug. "You're going to give this poor man the impression that we all have a good time here! So John, how's your dinner?"

"It's terrific," said John, "but I'm still waiting on the Beluga and the Dom Perignon."

"Well, sir, I'll see if the delivery man has arrived yet," said a grinning Carol. "Anything else I can get you in the meantime?" He shook his head, and she was off and running again.

"So you see, that's how you put that to work for you," continued Doug. "You figure out what you can't change, and you work with it, maybe changing it a little. I think that's where most folks get hung up. They think 'can't change that, so I won't change anything.' They just need to figure out how to work it."

John took another bite of steak. "How did you know that the bakery was something that would work for you? Did you do a lot of market research on the business?"

Doug chuckled and said, "Market research? Nah. I mean, I did start paying more attention to the shop during the times I came through here, to see what the activity was like. Sometimes I'd sit in there for a couple of hours, so I could hear what the customers were saying to the owners, and to each other. But beyond that, there's really nothing to research. After I overheard the owners say that they'd sometime like to retire and do something else, I approached them with the idea of buying them out."

"But how did you know it would work for you?" John waved an asparagus spear stuck on the end of his fork. "You didn't really have anything analytical to go on, did you?"

Doug looked at him intently, smiled, then said, "Rule #2, my friend, Rule #2!" He pointed dramatically across the room at another shiny brass picture frame.

**Rule #2: All you'll know is,
you'll never know, if you don't try.**

"I was just ready for a change." Doug shrugged his shoulders. "So that was my justification. I figured, what's the worst thing to happen? I'll just return to The City Area again and resume being a tech support rep. Why, even John Paul Jones agrees!" He turned and nodded at a framed quote hanging nearby:

"It seems to be a law of nature ... that those who will not risk cannot win."

(-- John Paul Jones, Revolutionary War hero)

Doug changed gears. "Say, listen John, I don't want to intrude on your entire dinner. But if you'll be around afterwards, come on into the bar. That's where I'm headed, and I'll buy you a nightcap." He stood up and stuck his hand out.

"Great, I'd like that," said John. "I'll see you in a while then." They shook hands and Doug headed for the bar.

Recap – The Journey of Revelation Begins
The 1st P: "Prepare"

The first phase of The 5 P's of Change is to mentally prepare yourself for a journey of change. To that objective, here are the first two Rules of Gumption, designed to start getting you into the right mindset to consider new horizons and possibilities.

Rule #1: Start with a small step – any step. Do something that starts you on your journey of revelation, whether it's researching something new, learning more about another industry, checking out a new location, fleshing out your true interests, etc. Don't worry about that step being the perfect starter. Take any step. Change steps later if you want to.

Acknowledge what you want to change, and be energized by the challenge. It won't necessarily be easy, but look upon it as a challenge to be met, a goal line to cross.

Also acknowledge what you can't change – live with it, work with it. Don't just complain about what you can't change. Find ways around it, to turn it into an asset or at least a motivator for yourself.

Rule #2: All you'll know is, you'll never know, if you don't try. Sometimes, you just have to take the risk, and go out and do it! All the research and analysis in the world will not necessarily point you to a clear answer.

When you get into the frame of mind where you realize that for some things, you just have to try it to see what happens, you'll be more open to taking that risk at the right time.

Starting to See the Light

"How was everything, John?" asked Carol as she saw John lining up his knife and fork on his empty plate.

"Terrible, can't you tell?" answered John with mock sarcasm and a smile. "Look at all the garnish I left!" He agreed to be tempted by the dessert tray, and asked for a cup of decaf coffee. After Carol recited the desserts, John decided on a mocha cheesecake. "Are these your homemade creations, Carol?" asked John with a grin.

"Actually, all of our desserts are fresh baked by the gentleman who was just sitting at your table," explained Carol as she pointed in the general direction of Doug and the bar. "And all of his baking is really, really good."

"Wow, I didn't even think of that," said John, "but I suppose I shouldn't be surprised. Doug looks like he's really enjoying himself, and seems like an easygoing guy."

"Yes, he is," agreed Carol. "Like some of the rest of us, moving here has been pretty good for Doug. I'll be right back with your dessert!"

As Carol walked away, John's thoughts again turned inwards. It appeared to be a nice place here, though he was sure it was a lot easier visiting than living here full time. The people he had met so far all shared the same experience of The City Area that he and his wife were part of. And they all made big changes, yet were enjoying themselves. But John didn't see relocation in the future for him and his wife, no way. We can't make any changes like this, he thought, we've got too many things we like in City Sprawl.

Then the stray thought from earlier in the evening hit him again – lately John and his wife hadn't been doing much, other than recovering from a hectic week. By Sunday afternoon, after some recovery, it was time to get ready to do it all over again Monday morning. Right around 5 or 6 o'clock on Sunday afternoons, he usually started to feel his stress level edging a bit higher again.

"Lost in thought?" Carol's voice broke his reverie. He had been staring at the wall.

"Lost in space, I think," said John. Carol put his decaf in front of him, followed by the plate with a slice of cheesecake. He continued, "Some of the things you guys have been talking about are resonating with issues my wife and I have been struggling with. Or maybe, in all fairness, my wife's the one who's been struggling, and I haven't been much help."

"What kind of issues?" asked Carol.

"Well, same kind – finding the right balance of work and personal life. Figuring out what's important to us. I'm not sure I even know exactly what our priorities are, except to make sure we make enough for the future, I guess."

"You know, we struggled with that, too," replied Carol. "Our problem became this – we weren't sure if we were headed for our objectives, or if we were on a treadmill."

"Well, I don't think we have the same flexibility you guys have. We're not in a position to up and move away from our home in City Sprawl," said John in a mildly defensive tone. "Even if I had any idea of where we'd go or what we'd do."

"But you don't have to relocate to create change for you and your wife," explained Carol. "You don't have to come to Gumption for change, all you have to do is bring gumption to your life in City Sprawl!" She grinned triumphantly.

John smiled back at her. "Easier said than done, you know."

"That's true, John, but what you need to remember is our Rule #3 over there," said Carol as she gestured to a brass frame hanging on another wall across the room.

Rule #3. Make a decision, dammit!

"You need to decide for yourselves, you and your wife, if you are going to look into making a change," said Carol.

"But I wouldn't even know what we'd change to," protested John. "How can I make a decision?"

"That's not necessarily the point," answered Carol, slipping into the seat across from John again.

"Remember what Greg told you about us? When we decided that our next step was to figure out a next step?" John nodded and Carol went on. "That's the decision we made, to set about figuring out what our next thing was going to be. If you and your wife think you need change, you need to make the decision to explore the alternatives."

"Sounds like the obvious, right?" continued Carol, warming to her point. "But you'd be surprised – a lot of people would rather not think about it, since they're not sure that they'd be able to come up with a different answer. Some of our friends didn't even want to talk about this kind of thing. I don't know, maybe they were afraid of becoming more depressed if they didn't come up with some kind of solution."

She laid her forearms on the table in front of her and lightly interlaced her fingers together. "Our feeling, Greg's and mine, was that we could always change our minds later, or if we didn't figure out a solution right away, we'd come back to it later. We figured that we'd figure it out! I guess we felt the same as Teddy Roosevelt over there." Carol pointed to another framed quote on the wall:

> **"In any moment of decision, the best thing you can do is the right thing. The worst thing you can do is nothing."**
>
> *(--President Theodore Roosevelt)*

John picked up his fork and dug into his cheesecake. "So, let me get this straight…"

"Oops, hold that thought," interrupted Carol, looking across the room. "Let me take care of some other folks, and I'll be right back!" She rushed off.

As John slowly ate his dessert, he thought about Carol's point. So she's saying that we don't have to yet decide where we're headed, he mused, before we've "made a decision." That decision could be to take action, to figure out if we want to make a change to our lives in the City Sprawl.

It's confusing, thought John as he put down his fork and took a sip from his coffee cup. We don't know what we might do, yet we'd be making a decision to do something. He tapped his fork lightly on the plate and shrugged to himself – maybe that's the revelation. Shelly and I would decide that we need to sit down and address the issues – that's the decision we'd be making, instead of ignoring the issues, continuing to live life day to day, and hoping it'll all work out.

He thought again about the argument they'd had before he left the house. With a couple of glasses of wine in him and a good dinner, he was feeling a lot mellower than before. And starting to feel just a little guilty too. Shelly was the one wanting to talk about the future, and he was the one wanting to wait until the perfect time. Well, there never is a perfect time.

John finished the last bite of cheesecake, and scraped the plate with the side of his fork. So if our decision is to address the issues, the possible outcome is a plan to change our lives – job-wise, location, or whatever. Or, maybe the result or conclusion we end up reaching is that everything is okay for now. He downed the last of his coffee.

"More decaf, John?" said Carol, startling John with her sudden return. "Oh, did I wake you up?" She laughed and refilled his cup.

"I was just thinking about what you said." John leaned back and looked up at the ceiling for a moment. "Let's see if I understand this now – you're saying that the decision you made was to see what alternatives there were, rather than to go on and not really think about it, right?"

"Right."

"And not knowing where that would take you, doesn't really have much to do with making that decision to investigate the possibilities, right?"

"Right again," said Carol. "It's a separate and future decision to go a certain way or not. We just had to come to a point where we needed to see what changes we might consider for our lives. Whether we decided to make a specific change is another, somewhat unrelated, decision. But if we hadn't treated the investigation of possibilities as a decision in itself, we'd probably still be sitting in The City Area, paralyzed by indecision. Or maybe just afraid of what we might uncover."

"And you're also saying that once you made the decision to seek alternatives, there's nothing that said you couldn't ultimately decide to leave everything the same," observed John.

"You've got it!" Carol laughed. "Say, are we getting you converted, or what?"

"Well, thinking, anyway," said John quietly, looking into his cup and stirring his coffee. He raised his head again. "So how did you go about looking at alternatives?"

"I've got one more table to finish up with, so let me do that, and I'll be back to answer your question." Carol darted off towards the other table. As John glanced around, he noticed that the dining room was almost empty, except for him and the other table's customers.

He looked at his watch. It was getting a little late, but not too late, he thought. On impulse, he took out his cell phone, flipped it open, then stopped. He thought for a moment, took a deep breath, then speed-dialed his home.

When his wife answered, John said, "Hi Shelly, it's me," but his tone was a lot more conciliatory than the last call, almost sheepish.

Mollified by his apparently mellower mood, Shelly listened as John told her briefly about the people he met over dinner, and how they had all moved from The City Area.

"I'm going to go into the bar for a little while to talk to this other guy, so I'll call you in the morning when I head out," John said.

"Okay," said Shelly, "talk to you tomorrow. G'night."

"G'night, dear," answered John. "Talk to you tomorrow." Back in City Sprawl, as Shelly hung up the phone, the "dear" that she heard her husband say was not lost upon her.

Carol reappeared at John's table. "More coffee, John? Anything else?"

"No thanks, Carol, just the check please," replied John.

"Actually, Greg and I decided that we'd be honored if you would be our dinner guest tonight. You're all set," Carol said with a smile. "It's always great to run into another guy from The City."

"Oh, no, you shouldn't do that!" exclaimed John. He took out his credit card. "Here, put it on my card!" After some back and forth about who should pay, John finally accepted the hospitality with profuse thanks. "I should pay you guys, for some of the things you've opened my eyes to," he said.

"Well, now let me finish answering what you asked earlier – how did we go about looking at alternatives?" Carol asked. John nodded.

"One of the first things we had to do was become students of change. That meant we had to start thinking only of change," said Carol, tapping the side of her head.

"We tried to think of everything that was opposite to what we had come to know or expect," she continued. "Then we'd dream about what our desired end result would be, ignoring any restrictions put on us by our present situation."

"But that's not that productive, is it?" asked John, putting his credit card back into his wallet. "After all, I could dream that I win the lottery, and then I can create the perfect life for my family, being able to afford whatever I need. But my chances of winning the lottery are probably slim and none."

"That's true," answered Carol, folding her arms. "But that's not the main thing we were thinking about. We were trying to figure out what we cared most about in life. Sounds corny, I know, but that's what we did. Greg and I talked about the kind of lifestyle we wanted, the kind of living environment we hoped for, the quality of life with our kids, and things like that. They were more abstract thoughts, rather than the things that money can buy."

"So maybe … you were trying to visualize the feel of things?" asked John, groping to understand.

"That's it!" exclaimed Carol, pointing at him. "A great description – we were trying to get an idea of what our perfect lifestyle would feel like."

John grinned. "Now the key question – what did it feel like?"

"Well, it was peaceful, we had control over our time, we were able to spend a fair amount of family time together, and so on. Oh, and no one-hour commute!" Carol laughed.

"All right, now answer this for me," continued John. "You've got this vision of peace and tranquility, and you're sitting in the middle of The City with very busy jobs. Doesn't that mean the inevitable and only conclusion is to relocate?"

"No, it doesn't," answered Carol. "From that feeling, we started to make some changes to our lives. Made more time for our kids, didn't worry as much about not getting that last thing done before leaving work, those types of things. We started shifting our priorities."

"But your priorities were always with your kids, right?" asked John, stroking the side of his jaw in thought.

"Do you have children, John?" she asked.

He shook his head and answered, "Not yet, but we plan to. If I ever agree to discussing it with my wife," he added sarcastically.

"Well," said Carol, "I hate to admit it, but I think Greg and I fell into the trap of expecting our kids to put up with the hectic schedules of our jobs, because we were doing what's necessary for them. And in so doing, we were asking them to be second-banana to the demands of our jobs."

John took a swallow from his coffee cup. "But I'm sure they understood perfectly, didn't they?"

"That's not the point – of course they had to understand," Carol said somberly. "What we had to realize was that Greg and I needed to be the ones to create the change. Change was not going to come because our kids demanded it."

At that moment, Greg walked up. "All done out here? Happy customers all on their way home?" He caught sight of his wife's expression. "Hey, what's up?"

Carol brightened up at her husband's arrival. "Oh, I was just telling John about us becoming students of change. And I was remembering how we had put the kids in the situation of being second to our jobs in The City, and then how we started to change those priorities."

"Yeah, we came to our senses," said Greg, smiling and giving his wife a quick squeeze around her shoulders.

"Okay, so being a student of change means that you're looking at what needs to change, to get to what you think is important in life, right?" summarized John.

"Yes," answered Greg, "then there's the next Rule of Gumption that goes hand-in-hand with that, and it's #4 over there." He pointed at the shiny frame on a rafter near the ceiling:

Rule #4. See the end result in your mind's eye.

"Ever read how pro athletes visualize the results of their efforts?" asked Greg.

"All the time," said John, "you read about how pro golfers visualize an entire shot even before hitting it – the ball flight, the curve, where it lands, how far it rolls, where it stops, and all that."

"Right. So we tried to do the same, Carol and I," said Greg, "except the imagery had to do with our lives."

"But that's what I still don't understand," John said with a confused look on his face. "You couldn't have visualized at that time owning a restaurant here in this town, right? How do you visualize what you don't know yet?"

Carol sat down across from John and smiled sympathetically at his puzzlement. "It wasn't that we imagined being here in Gumption, at least not in the early part of our thinking. Like I mentioned to you earlier, we concentrated on trying to see the end result of our family life being the way we wanted it to be. The quality of our time together, with our kids, what it felt like, what our interaction with our kids and each other would be like ..."

"In our case it was a matter of visualizing the emotion or feeling of things," added Greg, "and not so much the tangible things. We were visualizing how things were going to feel."

"Isn't that just what I said?" Carol looked up at Greg and glared at him. He grinned.

"I think ... I'm beginning to see this," said John slowly. "Your focus was on getting the feeling first, then later figuring out some of the more tangible things that get you to that feeling."

"That's about right," answered Carol. "Because if you think you can't start to visualize anything until you have every last detail worked out, then you probably won't get anywhere. And you won't have an end result to see in your mind's eye – because the end result will be whatever life delivers to you!"

"So what did you guys do, figure this out all on your own?" asked John. The couple chuckled at his words. "I'm sorry, not that I thought you weren't able to figure this out – I meant, did you talk to anyone else, or bounce your thoughts off your family? This is big, making the kind of change you guys did!"

"Sure is," said Greg. "And the answer is yes, we did share our thoughts selectively with certain people. But only certain people."

"Discussing this with some of those folks helped us continue to develop our thoughts as well," added Carol. "But I'll emphasize what Greg just said – we talked with only certain people."

"What do you mean?" John shifted in his seat.

"Hey what's the deal here, a meeting of the minds?"

They all looked up at the source of the interruption. Doug, the bakery owner, approached the booth. "I said I'd buy John an after-dinner drink, and I meant after-dinner, not before-breakfast!" He laughed and clapped John on the shoulder.

Greg grinned. "We'll be in there shortly. Carol and I need to tidy up around here. But I want to finish a thought with John real quick, then I'll send him over to you in the bar, okay Doug?"

"No problem," said Doug, "have to hit the men's room, anyway. See you in a bit!" He gave John a thumbs-up.

"Hey, don't forget to wash your hands, Dolce," called Carol, winking at John.

"Meaning?" Doug stopped and looked at her in mock indignation. "The sign in there says all employees are expected to wash their hands, and I'm not one of your employees!" He laughed and left.

Turning back to John, Carol continued, "So, where was I … oh yes, talking to only certain people. It's funny, when you talk about dreams and goals, different people have different reactions to it. You'd think most people would be encouraging, but we found that a lot of them were not."

"Not that they were discouraging," said Greg, "but it was more of a lack of encouragement. And when we're trying to figure out our lives, that's an uncertain enough thing to do. We didn't need to add someone else's insecurity or negativity to the mix."

Carol went on, "So we bounced ideas only off other people who had gone through major changes in their lives, because we figured that they'd be a better source of feedback."

"And there had to be a sense of mutual respect," added Greg, "because if that person didn't respect our desires to seek change, then we couldn't give much weight to his or her opinions."

"Did you talk to anyone in your families?" John gestured at both of them.

Carol looked at Greg. "A couple of them," said Greg. "My sister is someone I've always been able to talk to. And Carol's brother is good too. But not really anyone else in the family. I love 'em dearly, but they'd have the urge to dole out unsolicited advice."

"And they'd dole it out whether or not they had enough information!" Carol finished. Both she and Greg laughed.

"What kind of reactions were you getting from other people, the ones who you say you should ignore?" asked John.

"Oh, it was the whole gamut," replied Greg. "Some said, 'How can you do that – it's so much to change all at once?', and others said things like, 'Oh, I would never make such a change with two small children.' "

Carol said, "And we also heard, 'I can't imagine living anywhere else except The City Area. Do you know what you're getting into?' "

"So it's not like they were necessarily telling you not to do it," observed John, "but that maybe they couldn't see the need for change."

"Right," answered Greg. "But as I said before, you're already going through a period of great uncertainty trying to figure out what you want in the long run. There will always be naysayers out there, and plenty of them – why add to your confusion by listening to all of them, too?"

"You have to pick the right people to bounce your ideas and dreams off of," concluded Carol. "Like Gumption Rule #5, over there." Without even looking, she indicated a wall over her shoulder. John caught sight of the framed rule:

Rule #5. Listen to no one – except your advisors.

John grinned. "I see your point. Did you really listen to no one else?"

"In effect, that's what we had to do," said Greg. "We came to know who we could run things by, and who we didn't need to say much to – at least on this topic."

"Some friends would ask us how our thinking was going, and we'd just say that we were still trying to figure it all out," said Carol. "And, it's funny, but those friends would say, 'Yeah, told you, there's no better place to be than here in The City.' Well, that might be true for their situation, but that didn't mean it applied to us."

"So everybody's different," said Greg. "And everyone has their own view. You know what Clint

Eastwood as Dirty Harry said about this in one of his movies, right?" John shook his head. Greg pointed to his right, at a framed quote hanging in the booth across the way. "I'm sure you can figure out what the missing letters are."

> **"Opinions are like a__holes – everybody's got one."**
>
> *(-- Clint Eastwood as "Dirty Harry" Callahan)*

John read it and chuckled as Carol smirked.

"John, why don't you head to the bar while Greg and I finish up here," said Carol. "We'll join you in a few."

"Well, thank you again for dinner tonight," said John to the couple, as he stood up. "I really appreciate it, all the conversation and company, too!"

"Well, you're stuck with us tonight!" Greg laughed and pointed to the bar. "You'll get to meet some of the other characters of Gumption in there, whether you like it or not!"

John headed to the bar, as the couple busied themselves with closing the dining room for the night.

Recap – Starting to See the Light
The 2nd P: "Plan"

The second phase of The 5 P's of Change is to create a plan for your journey of change. See the possibilities, and start formulating the change. Here are three Rules of Gumption to keep in mind as you try to make sense of the jumble and come up with a plan.

Rule #3. Make a decision, dammit! Don't let the lack of complete details stop you from deciding that change is in the cards. Decide that you're going to figure out how to make a change, then …

Learn to become a student of change. Discover all the possibilities that change might bring. Let your mind roam to even consider things you might never have considered before. When you start to have some clues on what might be …

Rule #4. See the end result in your mind's eye. Like pro athletes do, visualize what things will be like as you make your changes. Don't just visualize the material things, try to imagine what everything <u>feels like</u> after changes occur. These could include the quality of your family life, day-to-day routines, your feelings, quality of your work life, etc. Use this vision to create a plan for getting there.

Start to develop some changes in your routine, in your priorities, or in your outlook on things. Turn these discoveries into steps that go into the plan that you're creating.

Rule #5. Listen to no one – except your advisors. Pick your advisors carefully, get their feedback, and ignore everyone else's opinions as you formulate and modify your plan. There are no shortage of naysayers out there, and everyone has an opinion, so don't go confusing yourself by trying to listen to everyone.

Executing the Plan

As John walked into the bar, he saw that the walls of the room, like the dining room, were covered with framed quotes, along with other paraphernalia. He recognized some of the wall hangings as more "Rules of Gumption" picture frames.

Doug, the owner of the bakery, caught sight of John entering the room. "Hey John, c'mon over and have a seat! What are you drinking tonight?"

John approached the table where Doug was seated. There were two others sitting around the table as well, and Doug waved him towards an empty chair.

As John smiled and nodded to the other customers at the table, he sat down and replied, "Well, I'll have an Irish coffee, then."

"Coming up! Hey Lloyd," Doug called to the bartender. "This is John. John, that's Lloyd. One Irish coffee for the gentleman here – and put it on my tab!"

Lloyd the bartender replied dryly, "Well, I'm glad to hear that there's one gentleman here tonight!" The group laughed.

"Hey John," said Doug, "say hello to some of the other upstanding residents of Gumption. This is Janine." John and the woman sitting at the table shook hands. "Janine is our local novelist, writing from this idyllic setting, and traveling the world on her book tours."

Janine laughed and said, "Well, hardly 'traveling the world,' but I am trying to get my novel published. Maybe then the book tours will happen."

The other man seated at the table said, "Yeah, she's aiming to be our local celebrity author."

Janine laughed again. She had eyes that seemed to sparkle. "That's the goal, to write from my home in this quaint little town, and travel when I need to. And in between, hang out with these characters here."

"Are you originally from around here?" asked John.

"No, I worked in healthcare in Big City in the Next State for many years. But I always wanted to be a novelist."

"And over here," said Doug as he pointed to the other man at the table, "we have Buck, our local CPA and financial consultant." Buck and John shook hands.

"What about you, Buck?" asked John. "Everyone I've met so far is from another town, are you, too?"

"Sure am," said Buck. "I was at a large CPA firm in Huge City in Another State."

"What did you do there, and what do you do now?" John inquired.

"Then, the usual CPA, public accounting thing," replied Buck. "And now, I still do CPA work, but I also have a financial consulting practice with clients nationally, mostly via the Web. You know how we accountants are, boring as hell." Everyone at the table laughed.

Janine said, her eyes sparkling again, "Oh, boring indeed! Here's our one and only Elvis impersonator on karaoke nights during high season!"

"Yeah, I had to learn 'Jailhouse Rock' in case I went to jail defaulting on my debts," said Buck with a grin.

He continued, "You see, John, I was a high flying, successful CPA, partner at a big firm in Huge City in Another State. Problem was, though I was great at accounting for other people's finances, I did a lousy job with my own. Had a weakness for the finer things in life, like BMW and Lexus cars, fancy vacations, and fine dining in restaurants."

"What happened?" asked John.

"Well, I just ran up a lot of credit card and consumer debt," answered Buck, "and got behind. And when you get behind, you never seem to make headway, because of those interest rates – it's like swimming upstream."

"So what did you do?" said John, sipping on the Irish coffee that Lloyd had put in front of him.

"Well, I quit cold turkey. Got rid of the Lexus for a cheaper car, laid off the vacations, and stayed in for dinner more. Made a big difference, and in less than a year, made a lot of headway towards getting out of debt. Then a funny thing happened."

"What was that?"

"My friends – my so-called friends, anyway – started calling me cheap. Said I wasn't any fun anymore, not going out drinking with them after work. Or deciding to bag out on going with them to Hawaii or Mexico on a resort vacation. I told them I couldn't afford it for awhile. They said I was getting boring. Imagine that — an accountant being called boring!" Buck laughed heartily.

"You'll hear more from Buck in a while," interrupted Doug, the bakery owner. "John, you should know that Lloyd, our inimitable bartender, also has his story, too!"

John looked over at Lloyd for his answer.

Lloyd, elbows on the bar, feigned being startled. "Who, me? Sorry, I was falling asleep, listening to Buck tell his story again." Everyone laughed. This was certainly a good-natured group.

"Okay, my story, let's see ... where to start?" said Lloyd, looking at the ceiling.

"How about where you're originally from?" prompted John.

"Well, I was a chemical engineer at a HighTech Valley company for about 9 years," Lloyd replied. "Got tired of the job, tired of things, wanted something new, so here I am! Any questions?" He smiled at John.

Grinning, John said, "So how did you come across this town, and how did you decide to switch from being a chemical engineer to tending bar?"

"Actually, tending bar is my night job," replied Lloyd.

"Yeah, he's not good enough for it to be his day job," called out Doug.

"Okay wise guy," said Lloyd, grinning broadly.

"What do you do as your day job?" asked John.

"I'm a winemaker," replied Lloyd. "I sell my wines through my Web site on the 'Net."

"That sounds pretty interesting!" exclaimed John. "How's business?"

"Not bad. I enjoy it, tending to the vines, and making limited batches of different wines. Probably won't become a millionaire, but hey, money isn't everything!" Lloyd smiled. "I could always work here to make some side dough."

"That depends on the level of customer complaints," said Greg, the restaurant owner, striding into the room. "Your continued employment is contingent upon our not getting too many reports of watered-down drinks!" The group laughed.

"I'd only water down your drinks!" Lloyd retorted.

Greg plunked himself onto a bar stool, between the table and the bar. He looked at the bartender and said, "Okay, give me a watered-down Coffee Keoki, then!" He turned to face the group at the table, leaning his back on the edge of the bar. "So what're you guys talking about?"

"I was just getting to know these fine people here," replied John, taking another sip of his coffee drink.

Greg looked at the others. "So you know that John's visiting us from The City and City Sprawl area, then?" The group's inquiring responses caused John to summarize again how he arrived in Gumption earlier that evening.

"What I think is interesting," continued John, "is that all of you are also from large metro areas, but you decided to do something different. Very different, it appears."

"Definitely," said Lloyd the bartender and winemaker. "When you reach a pressure point, sometimes you make a decision to relieve the pressure. Do you know about the Rules of Gumption?"

Greg and Doug laughed in unison. "Yeah, we've been lecturing him during dinner already! Amazing we haven't run him out of town yet," said Greg, looking at John.

"You don't have to worry about that," boomed Doug, "he's got a flat tire!" He laughed uproariously again.

John smiled and looked at the group. "Actually, it's been good, guys, I appreciate it."

"Well, if you think it's good stuff, then get ready for more," said Lloyd. "We live the Rules of Gumption, here in Gumption!"

"Well, I've been introduced to the first 5 rules, I think," said John. "What's next?"

"All right then, you know that you're at the point of formulating a plan, then executing it," said Lloyd. He put his hands palms down on the bar as he looked at John.

"Uh-oh, the professor is at the lectern, watch out!" warned Janine, the novelist.

Lloyd ignored her and went on, "So one thing to remember, as you're setting your plan for change, is to know how high to set your goals."

"When I was trying to figure out what I'd do if I ever left HighTech Valley," continued the winemaker and former chemical engineer, "I had to set goals at the right level. Not too high, so I'd never attain them, and not too low, which probably wouldn't amount to much change."

"So you had some idea of what you were going to do?" asked John.

"In general terms, I suppose. I knew that I was interested in wine, had always been. That's the beauty of being close to Valley of the Wines! And I figured that someday I'd want to be self-employed. So I started setting goals with those things in mind."

"But I'm still confused about this," said John in a slightly exasperated voice. "How can you go about setting goals for something you don't know yet?"

"Well, here's an example from my case," answered Lloyd. "I figured that within a certain timeframe, I needed to finish my research and understand the key issues of making wine. I already knew a bit about it, since it was a hobby of sorts, but I set a goal of becoming more knowledgeable about the field. I also had certain savings goals to reach, in order to be able to do this financially."

John nodded as Lloyd went on. "So if I set the goals too aggressively, then I'd never make it and probably give up. Like if I tried to reach the financial goal in 9 months – that's just not enough time on the salary I was making. Or, if I made the financial goal a 5-year goal, I'd also never make it because that was too easy, and I'd probably wander off track somewhere. You don't want to be too aggressive, and you don't want to be too lax."

Buck the CPA spoke up. "For me, the goal of reducing my credit card debt also had the same qualities. Too short a timeframe, I'd give up because it wouldn't be achievable. If I set too long a time, I'd probably put it off, thinking I had the time to procrastinate."

"And when I decided I needed to lose that extra weight," added Doug the baker, "I gave myself monthly targets of pounds to lose. At first, those targets were small, so I knew I could reach them. Then I gradually raised the bar." He looked at John and continued, "And as I told you earlier, once the quality of my life improved, losing the pounds seemed to get a lot easier."

John summarized what he had just heard. "So you guys are saying, set the bar high enough to get somewhere and stay motivated, but don't set it unrealistically high so that you end up giving up?"

"Right on," said Lloyd.

Buck spoke up again. "Having said that, there is a catch. You set your goals based on the best information you have at the time. But if you get new information, you may have to adjust your goals accordingly. So remember to question your wisdom regularly."

Lloyd nodded his head in agreement and said, "Yep, questioning your wisdom is a good thing, as long as you make it a sanity check, and not a downer."

Janine leaned forward to address John. "As I went through my plan to go from the healthcare industry to becoming a novelist, I had to adjust my sights at different times. It wasn't easy, questioning the plans I had put in place up to that point, but it certainly made me more sure of my direction. And each time, I knew more and more it was the right thing to do, for me, anyway."

Doug the bakery owner said, "The only thing I was questioning was whether there'd be enough donuts left over for me!" His booming laugh filled the room again.

"It can be tricky," continued Lloyd. "I mean, questioning where you are in your plan, not whether donuts are left over." He grinned at Doug. "You could be working your plan for change for a year or so, then find that you have to make some changes. Someone not so committed might just give up and say, ah, what's the use. But if you're committed to making a change, you'll find that you make the course corrections, and continue to execute. See that quote from the guy who brought about the concept of 'total quality' in business?" He pointed to another frame on the wall.

> **"It is not necessary to change. Survival is not mandatory."**
> *(-- W. Edwards Deming, American quality control expert)*

Doug grinned and said, "Yeah, no need to change, just get run over doing nothing." He looked up as two women entered the room. "Hey, look who's here!"

One of the women was Carol, Greg's wife, who finally finished closing up the dining room. "And look who I found outside," she said, indicating the woman with her. "Have a seat," she said to the woman, gesturing to an empty chair across from John. Carol perched on a bar stool next to her husband.

The woman sat down and caught sight of John. "Oh, hello again!" she said, smiling. She looked at the others and then back at John. "And you seemed like such a nice guy … how did you get mixed up with these characters?" Suddenly, John realized that she was the woman who checked him into his hotel.

"Oh, hello!" he said. "You work at the front desk at my hotel, don't you?" The entire group burst into loud laughter. John looked at them, a little bewildered. "Did I say something wrong?"

Carol said, "Yeah, Sara works at the front desk all right, and in the back office, and in the garden, and the housekeeping department, and the maintenance department, and…" They all laughed again.

Sara, the woman from the hotel, smiled at John and said, "Actually, I own the hotel. But, as these guys know, it's a small business, so I have to wear a few hats sometimes."

John grinned and said, "That explains it. So let me guess … you moved here from somewhere else, too?"

"Oh, you've been hearing everyone's story, have you?" she replied. "Right, I used to live in Major Metro City. I was the marketing manager for a large hotel chain."

"How did you come to move here?" asked John, reaching for his drink.

"Similar to what you've probably heard from everyone else," answered Sara as she gestured towards the rest of the group. "I used to come through here on vacation, on the way to the resort area. Always thought it was nice, but I guess I never did think of living here. That is, until about 5 years ago, when my husband and I started thinking that we needed a change."

"Does your husband work at the hotel, too?" John finished his now-cold Irish coffee.

"Mostly I'm the one working on the premises. He still does some consulting in his field, so he travels on occasion for projects." Sara looked up as Lloyd put a drink in front of her. "Thank you, Lloyd!"

"Sara, tell John the story of how you became the owner," said Carol, as she raised a frosty beer mug to her lips.

"Well, after my husband and I decided that we wanted to leave Major Metro City, I started to look at what we might do, where we might go. At the time, one of the other major hotel chains had a location here in Gumption, and was looking for a general manager. So I applied and got the job." She took a sip from her drink.

"After a couple of years," Sara continued, "the company decided not to continue the location, and was looking to sell the property. So my husband and I located financing, and negotiated a deal to buy the property from the company. And here we are!"

"How's it been going?" asked John.

"Just after we bought out, it was slow. That was part of the reason the company wanted to sell. When the economy started coming back gradually, occupancy started going up again, as more people headed back to the resort. Lately, we've been doing pretty well, but remember, our business in this town is cyclical. Busier in winter and summer vacation periods, and during fall foliage." Sara looked at the others. "Just like these other guys here, too."

"When you walked in, Sara, we were educating John about the Rules of Gumption," said Buck, the CPA.

Sara laughed and said, "Oh, no! My condolences, John. We don't mean to bore you on your first visit to Gumption, especially since you're only trying to get a flat tire fixed!"

"Actually I have to admit, it's been interesting," replied John. He paused and pondered the ceiling. "It's a new perspective and something to think about, given my life in City Sprawl."

"Ahem, well class is still in session," interjected Lloyd in mock seriousness. "Let's get to the next rule, #6 I believe. And I think Sara can give us her perspective on that one!" For John's sake, he pointed to where the rule was hanging.

Rule #6. Think "seize the moment, not "in a moment."

Sara said, "Yes, that did apply to us. When the company said they wanted to sell the location, we had to decide quickly whether we would be the ones to seize the moment, or face the uncertainty of letting fate take its course. And we didn't have a lot of time, so we couldn't put off the decision, either."

"How did you know it was the right thing to do?" asked John.

Sara pursed her lips, thinking. "Well, I don't know that we were sure it was the right thing. Then again, we didn't think it was the wrong thing, either. Sort of a matter of instinct and how it felt at the time, I guess." She shrugged her shoulders and looked at him with a smile.

Janine, the novelist, added, "Similar situation with me, when I got an offer from a small publisher to write. I figured, if not now, then when? I could probably always go back to healthcare. So I agree – 'seize the moment' is a good thing."

John frowned and thought for a moment. "Well, it's an interesting point. I must admit, sometimes I have a tendency to say 'well, let me think about it for a bit, and come back to it.' When I come back to it, it's gone. But then, I figure it must not have meant to be."

"That's true for some things," said Doug. "But sometimes you don't know if it's meant to be, unless you try to make it happen. So you seize the moment, and see if you're right."

He looked at his watch and said, "Say listen, I've gotta go soon. Unlike some of these night owls here, I have to rise with the cows to get fresh-baked goods on the tables of this town!"

"We've got one more rule for John in this group, don't we Doug?" asked Lloyd. "One more, on the topic of executing the plan, Rule #7."

John looked around the room for the rule. Carol caught his eye, and pointed to an area on the wall right over her head.

Rule #7. Small equals big.

"I'm not sure I understand that," said John, with a puzzled look on his face.

"This refers to the fact that sometimes the smallest things make the biggest difference," answered Lloyd. He was drying beer mugs with a towel.

"Not just sometimes," added Carol. "Lots of times."

"It's a matter of sweating the details," said Buck as he made a gesture of wiping away imaginary sweat from his brow. "The details are what really make things happen."

"When I was trying to make this novel writing thing happen," said Janine, "I had to pay attention to following up on the details of my plan. If I didn't, I'd probably still be waiting for it all to happen."

She continued, "I have friends who talk about making changes, but they start by doing only a couple of things, and assume the rest will follow magically. They don't follow up on any of the details that need to be done, and then they wonder why they're not getting anywhere. Then they give up."

"And that's how 'small equals big'," concluded Doug. "Do the small things right, and the big things happen." He stood up and smiled broadly at John. "Now I really do have to get my beauty sleep. John, it was a great pleasure meeting you. I hope we didn't bore you with some of our stories!"

"A pleasure meeting you, too, Doug," said John, rising to his feet and shaking hands. "I'll look forward to having some of your baked goods for breakfast tomorrow!"

"Good night, all, see you tomorrow!" said Doug, as he left through the bar exit door, to a chorus of good night's.

"All right, I guess I'm in deep enough," said John. "Are there any more Rules of Gumption?" The others laughed and nodded.

"Just 4 more, John!" said Buck, the CPA. "You might as well stay for the ending!"

"Okay, hit me with 'em, then," said John, sitting down again. "And another Irish coffee, decaf, if you don't mind, bartender! I don't want to be laying awake all night."

Lloyd laughed as he started to prepare John's refill. "All right, who else is up for one more?"

Recap – Executing the Plan
The 3rd P: "Pursue"

The third phase of The 5 P's of Change is to pursue your plan, but modify it if you need to as you learn new information. When executing your plan for change, know how high to set your goals. Implement your plan by identifying the goals you need to accomplish.

Set your goals ambitiously, yet realistically. Too high, and you won't get there. Too low, and you'll lose interest. Stay motivated.

Don't be afraid to question your wisdom regularly. It may be necessary to correct your course, or change your course. Check yourself to be sure that what you're trying to do still makes sense, and is still the right thing to do.

Two more Rules of Gumption to keep in mind during the Pursue phase:

Rule #6: Think "seize the moment," not "in a moment." If an opportunity presents itself, consider seizing it. Don't make procrastination or delay a habit. Certainly do the research you need to in order to make an informed decision, but know that you might not ever have "enough" information.

Most importantly, don't fall prey to "analysis paralysis", where one endlessly analyzes the possibilities and trade-offs, and never makes a decision.

Rule #7: Small equals big. The smallest things make the biggest difference. Sweat the details, and don't assume your desired outcomes will result from just a few things accomplished. Keep on it, make the small things happen, so big things can happen, too.

Sailing the Rough Seas

John looked around the room. Doug the bakery owner had left, but everyone else was still hanging out: Greg and Carol, husband-and-wife former residents of The City and now owners of the restaurant, sitting at the bar. Lloyd, behind the bar, winemaker, part-time bartender, and ex-HighTech Valley chemical engineer.

Around the table were Buck, former big-city CPA and now small-town CPA and financial consultant; Janine, the novelist and former healthcare worker from Big City in the Next State; and Sara, owner of the hotel, and former resident of Major Metro City.

As he sipped his second Irish coffee, John pondered the fact that all of these people had made significant changes in their lives. Changes that were driven by a need to balance their lives somehow, or a desire to just do something they dreamed of. Changes that they didn't necessarily know about for a long time in advance.

"So John, what's your story?" asked Lloyd from behind the bar, interrupting John's reverie. "I mean, are you thinking about personal changes? Is that why you're interested in the Rules?"

"No, I just stumbled upon the Rules when Carol and Greg started telling me about them while I was eating dinner out there," replied John as he gestured towards the dining room. He smiled at the couple. "Sort of a captive audience, I guess!"

They all laughed. Greg looked at Carol with mock disappointment and said, "Aw, and I thought he was going to say 'captivated audience'!"

"A bit to my surprise, I find the Rules interesting," admitted John, "but to answer your question, Lloyd – no, I wasn't necessarily thinking about personal changes when I arrived here. Tonight's discussion has been a thought-provoker for me, though."

He paused, shifted in his seat and moved his coffee cup, the others looking at him and listening. "You see, lately my wife Shelly and I have been struggling with some aspects of our lives, but I think we haven't been willing – or maybe able – to discuss this out loud. Or maybe I'm the one who's not been willing. We seem to have very little quality time together, as we rush around to make ends meet and plan for our future. We had a big argument about this as I left home for this trip."

"Do you have children, John?" asked Sara.

"No, not yet … we certainly hope to," John replied. He looked at Sara and shrugged his shoulders with his palms turned upwards. "But sometimes our schedules are so hectic, and we feel so worn out, that you almost don't feel like trying!" He grinned as the others chuckled.

"Let's not go there, now," cautioned Buck. "We don't know you well enough!"

"But, you know what I mean," said John, as several nodded in agreement. "So little time to catch your breath from an exhausting week … then suddenly, it's time to do it all over again!"

"So, you and your wife haven't really discussed any long-range plans?" asked Janine.

"Not really, I suppose," said John. "I mean, we've talked about our desire to start a family, but I can't say that we've sat down and tried to figure out the details like you guys highlight in your Rules."

He was silent for a moment, tapping the plastic swizzle stick against the lip of his coffee cup. John looked at the others, with a slightly embarrassed look on his face. "Um, I guess maybe I'm the one who's a little scared to talk about it. Like maybe we might not reach any good solution – then what would we do?"

"Hey, it sure is scary," said Janine. "You put yourself in a position to question the very nature of your life up to that point. Not easy to do, it takes … gumption, no pun intended."

The others in the room razzed her good naturedly. "Yeah, pun intended," said Buck sarcastically. "Gee, is that a new joke, Janine?"

"But you know what I mean, right?" continued John. He stared at the wall behind Lloyd. "It's like Shelly and I both know we need to talk about this, but we don't. Inside, we both know that if our schedules are as busy as they are now, what does that say for our schedules after we have a child? And where will we find the quality time?" Frowning slightly, he took a swig from his coffee cup.

No one said anything for a moment, as John put his cup back down on the table. He seemed lost in thought, again tapping the plastic stick against the side of his cup.

He looked up. "What makes this difficult is that we're surrounded by people who think everything's perfect. Well, maybe not perfect, but they think there's nothing wrong with the picture, because that's what everyone's doing these days – everyone's in the same boat."

John became more animated as he stared straight into his cup. "But everyone's not in the same boat! Shelly and I might have our own thoughts, and what's important to us might be totally different than what's important to other people we know!"

He raised his head again, and leaned back in his chair. "I think the uncertainty of not wanting to discuss the issues, coupled with having enough naysayers around us, is what causes us to put it off. Okay, it's me. I put it off. That is, I put off discussing the whole thing."

Again, the rest of the group was silent.

"Well, John, pay attention, because tonight is your lucky night!" announced Buck in a mock emcee voice, breaking the serious mood John's words had cast. Everyone laughed, and John managed a grin. "Our next 2 Rules are members of the group called 'Sailing the Rough Seas'!"

"Like we mentioned during dinner, there are so many people who have their own notions about what you should do," said Carol, leaning forward on her bar stool. "So when the ride gets a little bumpy – and it will from now and then – you have to be able to weather the storm and keep on going."

"What you have to do," added Buck as he pointed to John for emphasis, "is to remember that you're probably alone in your quest for change."

"We certainly had to remind ourselves of that time and again, didn't we," said Greg, looking at his wife. "We've heard our share of 'Why are you doing that?' and other, far less flattering remarks."

"But don't let it get to you," continued Carol. "You just say to yourself, okay, I'm alone in this, I'm okay with this, and to heck with everyone else!" She laughed and looked at John. "Of course, you wouldn't be alone, you'd be with your wife."

Janine said, "That wise gentleman's quote over there, says it all. Whoever he is …" She pointed at a framed quote near the end of the bar.

> **"The man who follows the crowd will usually get no further than the crowd. The man who walks alone is likely to find himself in places no one has ever been."**
>
> *(-- Alan Ashley-Pitt)*

"And who is he, pray tell?" asked Lloyd with a smirk on his face.

"Beats me," Janine shrugged, grinned, and took a sip from her drink.

John finished reading the quote and turned back to the group with a thoughtful expression on his face.

"Bottom line, John," said Buck, "don't give a hoot what the crowd does. Figure you're going to be alone, and do what you need to do. Remember I mentioned my so-called friends where I used to live? They were giving me a hard time about being no fun anymore, and being cheap. All because I didn't stay out drinking all night with them, or go on expensive golf vacations. I was definitely alone in my quest for change, but I'm sure glad I stuck it out."

"You'd think your friends would understand and respect your wishes," said John, shaking his head.

"Well, they had debt, too – a spending-oriented lifestyle. Maybe they thought that if I cut back, they should too, and they didn't want to. So it was probably easier to bad-mouth the change I was making." Buck shrugged, and moved his drink back on top of its cocktail napkin.

"And to my earlier point," Janine spoke up, "it can be darn scary. Hence Rule #8 of Gumption. Ta-daaa!" She gestured towards it, in the manner of a game show hostess, and in so doing, accidentally smacked Buck on the side of his head with the back of her hand.

Rule #8. Don't be afraid to be afraid – then get over it.

"Ow! I already know the rule, for Pete's sake," complained Buck, holding his head in feigned agony. "Do you have to literally pound it into me?" He pointed at John. "Besides, he's the new one here – pound it into his head!" Everyone laughed.

Janine ignored the interruption and continued, "Easier said than done, obviously. You have to face the fear of change by discussing the possibilities. It sounds like it's something you and your wife haven't done yet, John." She looked at him with a sincere expression in her eyes. "Maybe you should sometime," she said quietly.

John nodded slowly. "I know," he said. "Well, I know now. And you all make a good point, I think we – I – have just been afraid."

"It's okay to be afraid, then get over it and get on with things," said Buck, rubbing his temples. "Janine hit me in the head. I was afraid for a moment. Now I'm over it!" He snickered as Janine made a face at him.

Lloyd came out from behind the bar and sat on the stool next to Carol and Greg. "So while we're on this topic of 'Sailing the Rough Seas,' let's not forget that you're going to have to get used to hearing 'no' or 'can't' from some people."

"Isn't that the truth," said John in instant agreement. "I get some of that at work already!"

"You'll run the risk of hearing even more of it when it comes to your personal life," said Buck. He had finally stopped holding his head after the blow from Janine. "Surprisingly, it may come mostly from your family or close friends. Because somehow, they're more expert on your life than you are!"

John smiled and said, "Well, I can certainly relate to that. I'm doing pretty well as a region manager in sales right now, knock on wood." He rapped lightly on the table top in front of him. "I remember when I first decided to go into sales. I had experience in other functions, but wanted to add sales to my resume. When I happened to mention this to my parents, my mother said 'How are you going to do that? What if no one wants to buy anything from you?'"

The group laughed. John went on, "So I said, 'Mom, that's what selling is all about. You sell them on why they need the product. Then she said, 'But what if no one wants to buy? How will you make any money?' I thought, ah, forget it, Mom."

He looked around at the others. "Leave it to family to have undying confidence in your abilities, huh?"

Some in the group chuckled again. "When I first made the break to try getting my novel done," said Janine, "my parents had similar comments. 'You've never published anything before, how can you make a living doing that?' To which I said, well, there's a first time for everything, isn't there."

"You know what's funny?" said John, sitting forward in his chair. He looked up at Carol and Greg. "I think we talked about this before ... Over the years, some of the people who told me I couldn't do certain things, were the first to say 'I knew you could do it' after I'd succeeded in it." He sat back and looked at the others. "Works every time!"

"Yeah, everyone wants to jump on the bandwagon of a success, even if they didn't think the person had a chance," said Lloyd, taking a drink from his beer. He raised his glass in a toast. "Here's to success in spite of the naysayers!"

The group answered the toast, raising their glasses.

As she put down her glass, Sara the hotel owner looked at John and said, "The road to success is littered with potholes. So when you run into those potholes, you've got to keep the next Rule in mind." She pointed to a Rule visible just beyond the entrance to the bar.

**Rule #9. There will be setbacks
you can't explain. Forget them.**

"Sound logical enough," agreed John, nodding his head.

"But it's something you'll have to remind yourself about," said Sara. "The setback might be a supporter of yours changing her mind. Or a loyal customer who goes elsewhere. Or a client who you thought you did everything for, and who is still unhappy anyway. Maybe it's a dear friend who suddenly cuts off contact."

She shifted in her seat, leaned forward, and put her elbows on the table. "Too many people spend their time trying to find explanations or reasons for setbacks. And they get so bent out of shape searching for the reason, they forget what they're trying to accomplish in the first

---

place! Not only is it unproductive, because they'll never find an explanation, but it's also a waste of energy that could have been used to continue working towards the goal."

Sara sat back and folded her arms. "I should know – I used to do some of that early in my career. What a waste of time!"

Greg spoke up. "I think the key to this is a quick check to see if there's a reason, but if not, to just be able to move on. It's okay to be ticked off about a setback, but it shouldn't become all-consuming to find some logical explanation – especially if there really isn't one."

"Yeah, it's like a quote I read, attributed to Julie Arabi," said Janine. " 'Courage consists of the power of self-recovery.' "

"And who, pray tell, is Julie Arabi?" asked Buck, posing the question that everyone else was undoubtedly thinking.

Janine looked at them, thought for a moment, then shrugged her shoulders.

"Beats me," she said in unison with everyone else. Amidst the group's laughter, Janine winked at John, her eyes sparkling as she grinned. "She's someone who writes quotes, I guess. Anyway, it's a good point, you're sailing the rough seas, you have a setback you can't explain, and you show your courage and gumption through self-recovery and moving on with things."

"Makes sense," said John, nodding again. "I can't say that I've never succumbed to thinking in circles, trying to find a reason for something that happened. I guess I'd be better off just figuring out what to do next."

"Or figuring that you just go on doing what you were doing," said Lloyd, downing the last of his beer. "It doesn't necessarily mean that you change what you're trying to do. Sometimes you get hit with yogurt — you just wipe it off and go on!"

Buck added, "You might find it helpful to remember to occasionally look at things through the eyes of a child." He touched his forefingers to the corners of his eyes as he spoke.

John asked, "Now remember, I don't have children yet, but I assume that you mean to look at things simply?"

"And I don't have kids either," answered Buck. "That I know of, anyway," he added hastily. "I mean that you look at what's really important, in the overall scheme of things." He gestured inclusively to the group. "My friends with kids, including the fine parents here in this room, say that kids tend to not care about a lot of the things we adults get all torqued up about. And sometimes those things that really tee us off, I suppose aren't really that important in the end."

Lloyd said, "When I was still in the Valley, one of my friends told me that his kids made him put things in perspective. He'd tell me, 'You know, I'd come home all ticked off about some politics going on at work, and all my son wanted to know when I walked through the door was could I play with him now.' My friend said that actually helped him keep the b.s. in perspective, that it really wasn't that important after all."

Carol, who had been quietly sipping her drink for a while, spoke up. "Our kids really do that for us. Sometimes during high season things get a bit frantic around here, but when Greg and I get home, our kids just want us to read to them. So we really do get the perspective that any problems here are just work problems to solve, but in our kids' eyes, they're not that important. And I think that helps us tackle the rough seas when they do hit us, don't you Greg?" She looked at her husband.

"Definitely," said Greg, nodding in agreement.

"*Wait!*" cried Janine suddenly, startling everyone. "I just remembered the ultimate story about kids reminding you of what's important. I read about this in the sports news after it happened."

"You read the sports news?" asked Buck incredulously.

Janine made a face at him and went on. "Remember the 2006 U.S. Open in men's golf? Phil Mickelson, one of my favorite golfers, was at the 18th hole of the final round with a one-shot lead."

"Sure, what a finish – I saw it live on TV!" gushed John. "All he needed was par for the win, bogey for a playoff. He hit a bad drive, tried to go for the green on the second shot, then ended up double-bogeying into a tie for second place. He was devastated."

"Right," said Janine. "But it's what happened afterwards with his family that I really think makes the point we've been talking about."

She leaned forward in her chair, animatedly continuing the story. "About an hour after Phil's misfortune on the 18th, he arrives back at his rental house where his wife and three kids are waiting. He opens the door, and gets mobbed by his family."

"His 7-year-old daughter asks, 'Did you win, Daddy?' Phil answers, 'No.' Then she says, 'I'm sorry. But second is soooo good. Second is wonderful. ... Do you want pizza?' "

Janine laughed with her eyes screwed shut. "I think that is such a cute story! I loved it when I read about it!" She opened her eyes. "Just think, Phil loses the biggest tournament of his dreams, and all his daughter wants to know is if her daddy wants pizza. Talk about moving on!" Janine laughed again.

"That is a great story," agreed Sara. "It really seems to be true that children rarely if at all dwell on setbacks." She looked at John and continued, "My children are grown now, but when they were little, setbacks didn't seem to faze them one bit. They either kept trying, or they went on to the next thing."

"So, what you guys are telling me is," concluded John, "if it's not that important, fix it, get over it, forget about it, get on with it, or ignore it, right?"

"You got it," said Greg. "And one more thing you should remember ..." He looked at the others as he continued, "Speak up if you disagree, guys, but I was going to remind John that the Road to Gumption sometimes takes you through places you don't want to be."

The others nodded and murmured in agreement. John looked at Greg and raised one eyebrow questioningly.

Greg answered the unspoken question. "You see, John, it's not just the setbacks you have to learn to move on from. There may be times where you just plain wonder if you took a wrong turn, and you really just don't want to be where you are."

Greg folded his arms and continued. "What you have to remember is that sometimes you can only get to where you want to go, by going through some place where you don't want to be. It could be an assignment that you don't really want to do, or some job you don't really like. But if you see the long-term end result in your mind's eye like Rule #4 says, you'll realize that this is something you have to do to get to your goals."

Putting her hand on her husband's arm, Carol added, "And you'll be able to live with that short-term drudgery that much better, because you'll know that you're only passing through on to bigger and better things. You guys agree?" She looked around at the others.

Everyone else nodded their agreement, and John slowly nodded his understanding as the words sank in.

Suddenly, a loud clanging sound rang throughout the room. Startled, John straightened up and realized it was Lloyd with a big grin, ringing a ship's bell on the wall behind the bar.

"Ahoy mates, last call!" called Lloyd. "I need to get my beauty sleep, too!"

"Wouldn't make any difference if you slept like Rip van Winkle," said Buck sarcastically, "you'd still be ugly." He dodged a coaster that came sailing his way.

Everyone was fine with their drinks. Lloyd started to close things up behind the bar. Sara looked at John and said, "Only 2 more Rules to go, #10 and #11! Then you'll know it all!" She smiled.

"And we'll hold your graduation ceremony!" said Buck. The group laughed.

Recap – Sailing the Rough Seas
The 4th P: "Persevere"

The fourth phase of The 5 P's of Change is to persevere in spite of rough times. Any journey of change is filled with setbacks, disappointments, and discouragement, but also with hope, progress, and triumphs.

You may find yourself alone in your quest for change. There will be many who will not share your views, your ambitions, your hopes, your dreams. Some may feel jealous, threatened, uncaring, or simply uninterested.

Just keep at it. You're going to hear words like "no", "can't", and other negative thoughts, so you might as well get used to it. When the seas get a little rough, here are 2 Rules to keep in mind.

Rule #8: Don't be afraid to be afraid – then get over it. Change can be scary, sometimes very scary. So, go ahead, be afraid, get the adrenalin pumping, put your head down, get over it, and keep going.

Rule #9: There will be setbacks you can't explain. Forget them. Don't worry about trying to find an explanation. Quickly check to see if you can discover why the setback happened, but if there is no reason, then move on. Don't waste time or energy trying to reason why, or lament over what might have been. Don't waste energy trying to find logic or reason for the negative events.

(continued on next page ...)

Recap – Sailing the Rough Seas
The 4th P: "Persevere"

(... continued from previous page)

Try using a child's perspective to help you move on. Children rarely dwell on setbacks; they just try it again or move to the next thing. Sometimes what really ticks off adults can be unimportant from a child's view. So it may actually not be that important, even from an adult's view. And if it's not, you move on, too.

Remember, the Road to Gumption sometimes takes you through places you don't want to be. Stay focused on why you're on the Road and how it gets you to your long-term goals.

It's not unusual to find that the only way to get to where you want to go, is to go through that less-than-desirable place, whether it's a boring assignment, making less money, or a job that's not particularly you. If you know what you need to get out of the short-term temporary situation, you'll be able to pass right through and get on to bigger and better things. Keep the end goal in mind.

Staying in the Sunlight

As Lloyd readied the bar for closing, John turned back to the rest of the group and asked, "Okay, you've taken me through the first 9 Rules of Gumption. What are the remaining 2, Sara?" He looked at the woman who owned the hotel.

Sara said, "Well, the last two Rules are part of the phase we call 'Staying in the Sunlight.' We all know it's hard making changes, working towards new objectives and things like that. We also know that sometimes we can be our own worst enemy, thinking negative thoughts or having doubts about ourselves. So this phase is all about how to keep as positive a perspective as possible. I really like the quote from Ben Franklin over there." She gestured towards a picture frame hanging to the right of the bar.

> **"Do not anticipate trouble, or worry about what may never happen. Keep in the sunlight."**
>
> *(-- Benjamin Franklin)*

John read it, nodding his head. "That's a great thought. I'm certainly guilty of worrying about things that haven't even happened yet."

"Aren't we all," agreed Sara. "You want to anticipate what might come up, so you know what you're going to do, but you don't want to worry yourself silly about every possible thing that might happen. Rule #10 reminds you about this. It's out there in the dining room somewhere." She waved in the direction of the restaurant tables.

"There it is," said Carol, pointing. "You can see it just above the table in that end booth, there."

Rule #10. Worry smart.

"Hmm," said John, "meaning …?" His voice trailed off.

"Meaning you only do what we call productive worrying," Buck interjected. "Let's say it's 3 in the morning, and you're laying awake worrying about something. If there's something you can do about it right at that moment, then get up and do it. But if there's nothing you can do, and you've already figured out your contingencies, then don't worry about it."

"Now c'mon," protested John, "that's a lot easier said than done." He waved his hand in mock skepticism.

"Don't be a naysayer, John!" Buck countered with a grin.

"It is easier said than done," agreed Janine. "But you have to train yourself to be able to do that. I did — wasn't easy though, that's for sure." She downed the last of her drink and paused to collect her thoughts. "When I first decided to quit my job and spend full time writing my novel, I started getting really anxious about, what if I

---

couldn't publish the book, or what if the book didn't sell, or what if whatever came to mind."

She pushed her chair back slightly and crossed her legs. "I'd be laying awake at night thinking these crazy what-if thoughts. Finally I realized that these what-if scenarios were irrelevant, if I didn't even have a book to try to get published. So I started to focus on finishing the manuscript, not on what might or might not happen after I finished."

Janine touched John on his forearm and continued, "I had to train myself to not worry about the future, because my current job was to finish the manuscript. Then, after getting the draft done, I can lay awake all night worrying about whether it'll sell or not!" She laughed.

"From the sound of things," said John, "I'm sure you'll realize your dream."

"Well, that's the point of Rule #10," answered Janine. "I don't know if I'll reach my dream or not, but when I lay awake worrying, I realized that I won't know anything about whether my book sells, until I finish the book first! So worrying about the future was definitely not productive worrying, as Buck would say."

"I have some clients for my financial consulting business who live in other parts of the country," said Buck, "and once in awhile I wake up at night thinking about their issues. But unless there's something I need to get up and do right then, I just put it out of my mind and go back to sleep."

John looked at them in mild disbelief. "I just don't see how you can turn it on and off, though."

Lloyd looked up from washing glasses behind the bar. "It's like Janine said, you have to train yourself to do this. You can't keep worrying about things that may never happen." He straightened up and dried his hands with a towel.

"For example, I could lay awake," he continued, "and worry about whether Greg's going to fire me as his bartender, and hire somebody else instead. But since I already know what I'd do if that happened, I don't worry about it anymore." He looked at Greg and smirked, as the others laughed.

Greg feigned deep thought and then revelation. "Hey, that's an idea! Maybe we can then get some more customers in here who order more than just ice water!" He jolted forward a little as his wife Carol hit him lightly on the back of his head.

"Then again, I guess we'll stick with you, Lloyd," he said with a chuckle. "Just start charging for the ice."

Still skeptical, John said, "Well, that's certainly a Rule that makes sense, but it seems pretty hard to do."

"Hey, life is hard," said Buck, "then you move to Gumption." He grinned wryly. "But seriously John, you'd be surprised at what you can do, once you train yourself to do it."

"While we're on the Rule of worrying smart, I want to mention one other thing," Greg said, addressing

John. "When you're making changes, you're probably not going to get it right the first time, or every time."

"Meaning, if you screw up, don't worry about it!" exclaimed Sara. "I don't speak from personal experience, of course…" She smiled to a chorus of the others muttering "Yeah, right".

Janine looked at John and said, "The key here is being patient, and learning from your previous mistakes. I've found that sometimes you have to go down the wrong path first, before you stumble on the right path."

"Interestingly enough," Carol said from her perch on her bar stool, "there are times when you'll find that the wrong path gives you the information and learning you'll end up needing, when you finally go down the right path."

Greg leaned back and put his elbows on the bar behind him. "It happened to us, when we first took over this restaurant, and were trying to figure out the right formula."

"But how do you know you're not just spinning your wheels at some point?" asked John.

Greg looked at him thoughtfully. "Great question," he responded. "To be honest with you, sometimes you can't be sure."

"It's probably a matter of personal feeling," offered Lloyd, almost finished with his work behind the bar. He came around to the table, started to collect the glasses, and wiped the table. He looked around at the others, sitting watching him. "Gee, thanks for helping, but I can handle this myself!"

"That's why we pay you the big bucks, dear," said Carol.

"Yeah, right. And this is why I'm an Internet-based wine seller," Lloyd grinned as he went behind the bar again. "Anyway, as I was saying John, it's probably a matter of feel, as to whether you're learning from your mistakes or spinning your wheels. I think if the general feeling is that you're making progress and headed in the right direction, then you're doing okay. If it looks like you're hitting setback after setback, then maybe you step back and see if it's still making sense."

"There will be times when you feel like throwing in the towel," agreed Sara. "The first year or so after we bought the hotel, there were times we felt like that. But we stayed in the sunlight, so to speak, by remembering that it's no big deal to make some mistakes. Anyway, you learn far more from slip-ups than if everything went smoothly from the get-go."

Janine piped up, "Yeah, just check out the quote from Samuel Beckett, over there." She pointed to a frame hanging next to the dart board on the wall opposite the bar.

"Ever tried. Ever failed. No matter. Try again. Fail again. Fail better."

(-- Samuel Beckett, 20th century author)

"So what's left, one more Rule?" asked John, glancing at his watch. "I really do appreciate the insight you've been giving me, but I don't want to keep you guys all night!"

Lloyd finished putting away the last of the glasses, wiped his hands and came out from behind the bar. As he started to shut off the lights in the bar, the group stood up from their chairs and headed towards the dining room.

Janine linked her right arm through the visitor's left arm, and as they passed through the entry back into the dining room, said "Before we get to the last Rule, another trick for you to stay in the sunlight. We've been talking all night about how to deal with the setbacks and negative thinking. As you make your way down your own Road to Gumption, celebrate some successes, even if they're small ones."

"Try to do that whenever you can," said Buck, as most of the group stood gathered around informally in the dining room. Carol and Greg were shutting off lights in the kitchen and in other parts of the dining room.

"No success too small to celebrate!" added Sara. "After all, if you don't celebrate them, who else will?" She gestured for emphasis. "Remember, you're all alone most of the time!"

John nodded his head. "Makes sense…"

"It absolutely makes sense," echoed Greg, walking back from the kitchen area. "But you have to remember to do it."

Carol returned to the group from the other direction. "And sometimes you get so busy fighting fires, you forget to celebrate those successes. Or you take the little successes for granted. Fact of the matter is, you go too long without celebrating anything, it gets to be one long road."

Buck said, "That's sometimes how even success can become a treadmill, when you don't take any time to celebrate what you've accomplished."

"What do you do to celebrate?" asked John. "Anything in particular?"

"Depends on how big the success is," replied Lloyd. "I work all day on my winemaking business, before coming to work here. Sometimes when I've done something I think is worth celebrating, I might take the afternoon to play 9 holes of golf, or decide to take part of a morning to go for a bike ride. Something to treat myself."

He grinned and continued, "Now, when I get that first really big wine supplier contract, I'll really celebrate by buying a nice dinner!" He looked around the room. "Aw shucks, just realized that the nicest place in town is here. That would be like coming to work!" He laughed.

Carol smiled and said, "When you get that contract, we'll buy you a nice dinner here, how's that?"

John was looking around the room, scanning the walls. "So where's the last Rule, #11?"

The group started to move towards the front door, as Greg turned off more lights in the main dining area.

Light from the street lamps outside shone through the windows of the front door. Janine reached the door first, opened it, stepped through, and stood there holding the door open for the others to follow.

As Buck got to the doorway, he indicated the final brass picture frame just to the left. He tapped the glass with his finger. "Here's your final Rule, John."

Rule #11. Trust yourself. Believe in yourself.

John paused for a moment to read the Rule, then followed the others out the front door. Carol brought up the rear, turned out the last light, and locked the front door behind her. All seven of them gathered on the short walkway to the parking lot, a few steps from the restaurant's front door.

"Trust myself and believe in myself, huh?" repeated John.

"Yes indeed," said Buck. "Just like Sara said about celebrating success, if you don't trust and believe in yourself, who else will?"

"You're the one who will know the most about what you're trying to do, where you're trying to get to," said Janine. "Or, in your case, you and your wife. So, you have to believe in yourselves, that you'll make what you want to happen, happen."

Carol put her arm around her husband's waist. She said, "I think it's easier when you have someone who can believe in you, and you can believe in them. Even through some of the roughest seas, Greg and I always felt that we trusted ourselves to do the right things."

"When you trust yourself, it doesn't mean that you're not going to make mistakes," added Sara. "It just means that you trust yourself to keep heading in the direction you've chosen. Or the one that you and your wife have chosen."

"Well, the direction I've chosen is straight to my bed," said Lloyd with a big yawn. "Good night, all!" He turned to John with a big smile. "A huge pleasure meeting you tonight, John! All the best to you, and I hope you get your car fixed tomorrow."

John shook hands with the Internet wine seller and part time bartender. "The pleasure was really mine, Lloyd, and thanks very much for all your advice. I always read that bartenders have lots of insight for their customers!" They both laughed, and Lloyd headed to his car.

"Well, we're off too," said Greg. "Good luck to you, John, and give our regards to The City!" John shook hands with Greg, and got a quick hug from Carol.

"Thank you both very much, too," said John. "And also for my dinner tonight." The couple waved and started towards their car parked nearby.

"Will we see you tomorrow?" asked Janine, standing with Sara and Buck.

"Probably not," John said apologetically. "I'm going to try to get on the road as soon as my car's fixed. I'll have to reschedule all of my morning customer visits." He smiled gratefully. "It really was terrific, meeting all of you. Thank you very much for sharing your stories with me tonight!" John shook hands with each in turn.

Buck and Janine went to their cars, parked next to each other in the now empty parking lot, as Sara turned to John and said, "Headed back to the hotel? I'll walk over with you."

"That would be my pleasure, ma'am," replied John. He turned and waved good-bye to the other two as they each drove away. He and Sara started off on the short walk across the parking lot, back to the hotel.

Recap – Staying in the Sunlight
The 5th P: "Positive"

The fifth and final phase of The 5 P's of Change is to stay positive. It's easier than you think to get yourself down, with self-doubts or premature worrying. Stay in the sunlight, as Ben Franklin once said. The last 2 Rules of Gumption to remember:

Rule #10: Worry smart. Don't worry about things that haven't even happened yet. Be productive in your worrying. If you're worrying about something, and you can do something about it now, then do it. If there's nothing you can do about it now, then forget it until the time arrives when you can do something.

Remember that you may not get it right the first time. And probably not every time, either. Mistakes will happen; they're part of the process, don't sweat it. Work them through, learn from them, and keep heading towards your goal. You learn more from mistakes, anyway.

And remember to celebrate even small successes. They're just as important as overcoming mistakes. Treat yourself when something is worth celebrating. Even little things are worth celebrating. Every small success brings you that much closer to your goal.

Rule #11: Trust yourself. Believe in yourself. You know what you're trying to do, and you know you're the one to make it happen. Trust yourself, and really believe that you're going to reach the goals and changes you've set for yourself. They may not happen right away, or exactly according to your desired schedule. But your belief in yourself ultimately <u>will</u> translate to realizing your goals.

Epilogue

John got up early the next morning, and packed up his things. As he went downstairs to check out, he saw Sara at the front desk again.

"Thanks again for all your help," he said warmly to the hotel's owner. "I really appreciate the perspectives you all gave me. Really opened my eyes, in some ways I hadn't even thought of."

"Well, good luck to you and your wife," Sara said. She shook hands with John. "I hope you both find the journey of change you're looking for!"

"Me too," he agreed. "I think when I get home after this trip, Shelly and I will have some of those down-deep discussions that I've been avoiding."

John left the hotel, headed for the repair shop, and found it open for business. After telling the owner, Todd, what he needed, he sat down to wait. He flipped open his phone, and speed-dialed his wife's cell phone. She hadn't left for work yet.

"Hi Shelly, it's me," he said when she answered.

"How are you, John?" she asked. The tension from their argument the day before seemed to be gone, but both avoided any mention of it. Shelly and John briefly brought each other up to date on what they did the night before. John didn't mention anything about what he learned from the residents of Gumption, only that he had a nice time meeting all of them.

"I'll be on my way again shortly, they're fixing the tire right now," said John.

"Okay, dear, I'll talk to you tonight. Have a good day and drive safe," said Shelly. The significance of the word "dear" wasn't lost on John. Perhaps he would be allowed back in the house again by the end of the week.

He ended the call and started making some other calls to his customer accounts to reschedule the morning appointments. None were able to commit to a specific time in the afternoon, but they told him he was welcome to stop by anyway.

As John slipped his phone back into his pocket, his thoughts turned again to the discussions of the previous night. He thought about the 11 Rules of Gumption he had learned, and about the changes that the people he'd met had made to their lives.

He wondered if he and Shelly would be able to figure out their directions, what they'd really like out of life. They certainly needed to do a lot of thinking and talking. He hoped he could do his part to contribute to that process.

"Sir? Your car is ready," said Todd, interrupting John's train of thought.

He stood up. "Oh, thanks, I'm all set?" He had paid for the repair earlier.

"Yes sir, have a good trip."

John got into his car, started it up, and headed out of Gumption, back towards the freeway. As he drove down the tree-lined road, his thoughts returned once again to Shelly, their family plans, their jobs, and their lifestyle.

Before long, John approached the freeway entrance ramp. He stopped at the Stop sign, reading the ramp signs. Big City in the Next State, where he was headed, to the right. The City, where he and Shelly lived, to the left.

John put the car in motion, ready to continue his interrupted trip. Then on sudden impulse, he spun the wheel and abruptly took the left ramp, tires squealing as he accelerated. He merged onto the freeway, and speed-dialed his wife's phone.

"Hi honey, it's me again. I'm coming home. Got any lunch plans?"

The 11 Rules of Gumption™
and The 5 P's of Change™

Prepare: *The Journey of Revelation Begins*

Rule #1. Start with a small step, any step.

Rule #2. All you'll know is, you'll never know, if you don't try.

Plan: *Starting to See the Light*

Rule #3. Make a decision, dammit!

Rule #4. See the end result in your mind's eye.

Rule #5. Listen to no one – except your advisors.

Pursue: *Executing the Plan*

Rule #6. Think "seize the moment," not "in a moment."

Rule #7. Small equals big.

Persevere: *Sailing the Rough Seas*

Rule #8. Don't be afraid to be afraid – then get over it.

Rule #9. There will be setbacks you can't explain. Forget them.

Positive: *Staying in the Sunlight*

Rule #10. Worry smart.

Rule #11. Trust yourself. Believe in yourself.

To share your story of your own journey on the Road to Gumption, visit:
www.RoadToGumption.com

About the Author

Gary Lim, M.A., is the President of Aurarius LLC, a strategic and business management consulting firm he first founded in San Jose, California, then relocated to Upstate New York. In addition to Aurarius, he founded CEO PrivateLine, and is a co-founder of HealthcareBusinessOffice LLC.

An experienced speaker from the platform, Gary has spoken live to audiences ranging in numbers literally from 2 to 2,000 people. Cumulatively over his career, his speaking engagements have been attended by over 10,000 attendees, through keynote speeches, conference workshops, corporate/executive seminars, product launches, and training courses.

Gary is also Visiting Professor of Entrepreneurship at the State University of New York, College of Environmental Science and Forestry, located in Syracuse, New York. He was previously the inaugural Managing Director of the entrepreneurship program at Syracuse University.

His educational credentials include a Bachelor's degree earned *cum laude* from Princeton University in electrical engineering and computer science. Later in his career, he earned a Master's degree in organizational management from University of Phoenix.

Gary's experience and skill set are focused in the areas of helping companies, organizations, and individuals achieve even higher levels of performance. This is accomplished by creating and applying the right strategies and focusing implementation on key critical issues. In his work with client companies and seminar attendees, Gary is often referred to as being one of the best at assessing complex situations, distilling them to a few key issues, and creating solutions that are clear and concise.

After a corporate and entrepreneurial career that spanned twenty years in the region of the San Francisco Bay Area known as "Silicon Valley", Gary and his wife took their own journey down the Road to Gumption. The process of self-examination they went through formed the genesis of the book *The Road to Gumption*. The result was relocation to Upstate New York when Gary accepted a position at a major university, doing something quite different than he had ever done in his business career.

The journey continues, and currently Gary divides his time between consulting, speaking, writing, teaching, managing multiple ventures that he co-owns with his wife Judy, and evaluating new business opportunities. Being on the Road to Gumption has also enabled the couple to set aside quality time for LOAFing around with their young daughter.

For more information on Gumption™ workshops, custom seminars, or volume purchases of this book:

Book Web site:	www.RoadToGumption.com
Consulting Web site:	www.AurariusLLC.com
Email contact:	info@RoadToGumption.com
Phone contact:	315-885-1532 (direct)

Summary information on Gumption™ workshops appear on the next two pages.

GUMPTION™ WORKSHOPS

Two Gumption™ workshops are based on the book *The Road to Gumption: Using Your Inner Courage to Balance Your Work and Personal Life*. The public seminar is "Weekend of Gumption™," and the custom onsite workshop is "The Road to Business Gumption™".

Weekend of Gumption™

Taking place on select Saturdays in different cities throughout the U.S., *Weekend of Gumption* allows attendees to immerse themselves in their own journeys on the Road to Gumption, with author Gary Lim facilitating and coaching.

During a concentrated Saturday session, participants will apply the Rules of Gumption specifically to their own needs, in a private and supportive environment.

- Start to develop your plan for your journey.
- Ask the questions you've been hesitant to ask.
- Float the ideas you've been afraid to run by friends and family.
- Freely express, then address, your doubts about your journey,
- Get suggestions, help and advice on implementation.
- Receive honest and objective feedback.

No naysayers here! Everyone who attends wants to travel their own Road to Gumption to reach their goals. Small sessions (10-20 attendees) allows high levels of interactivity. After the workshop ends, attendees also receive 3 months of unlimited email dialogue with the author, as they start their journey down their Roads to Gumption.

Included with each *Weekend of Gumption*:

- Intensive and focused Saturday workshop session
- All seminar materials

- Continental breakfast and refreshments
- Unlimited post-workshop follow-up via email dialogue with the author for 3 months (couples receive 6 months)

Visit the Web site for full details and currently scheduled seminar cities:

www.RoadToGumption.com/workshops.html

The Road to Business Gumption™
(Custom Onsite Workshop)

The Road to Gumption is actually a story about creating change in situations where one might not know exactly where to begin. Because this is a dilemma that many corporate and not-for-profit organizations face, we offer the custom seminar *The Road to Business Gumption™: Creating Change in Your Organization*.

In a customized, half-day onsite session, your management and associates will apply The 5 Ps of Change™ and the Rules of Gumption™ to their organizational issues and priorities. This methodology tends to create a greater openness to a culture of change, making the process of executing change less mystical and more focused.

The workshop, facilitated personally by author Gary Lim, can be held at your corporate location, offsite meeting, industry symposium, or other conference venue. Contact the author to request a no-obligation detailed quote:

Phone: 315-885-1532

Email: info@RoadToGumption.com